The Economic Life of Refugees

_____

Karen Jacobsen

_____

Kumarian
Press, Inc.

The Economic Life of Refugees

Published in 2005 in the United States of America by Kumarian Press, Inc., 1294 Blue Hills Avenue, Bloomfield, CT 06002, USA

Production by Jennifer Boeree, Scribe, Inc.
Interior design by Andrew Brown, Scribe, Inc.
Copyedited by Reyna Howkins, Scribe, Inc.
Proofread by Susan K. Hom, Scribe, Inc.
Index by Herr's Indexing Service
The text of this book is set in Adobe Garamond 10/12

Printed by McNaughton-Gunn, Inc.

∞:The paper used in this publication meets the minimum requirements of the American National Standard for Information Sciences—Permanence of Paper for printed Library Materials, ANSI Z39.48-1984.

Library of Congress Cataloging-in-Publication Data
Jacobsen, Karen.
    The economic life of refugees / by Karen Jacobsen.
       p. cm.
    Summary: "Explores the economic life of refugees in protracted situations in a variety of settings: in camps, in urban areas and in third countries in the West" —Provided by publisher.
    Includes bibliographical references and index.
    ISBN 1-56549-204-8 (pbk. : alk. paper)
    1. Refugees—Economic conditions 2. Refugee camps. 3. Economic assistance. 4. International relief. I. Title.
HV640.J327 2005
330.9'0086'914—dc22

                                                    2005004339

14 13 12 11 10 09 08 07 06 05   10 9 8 7 6 5 4 3 2 1   First Printing 2005

The Economic Life
of Refugees

Contents

Preface

This book is about the thousands of refugees in protracted situations who survive and even thrive after their initial flight across borders: having come through danger, they find opportunity. Common to almost all refugees is destitution resulting from their flight experience, paired with a strong desire to support themselves by pursuing livelihoods. The ways in which they do this, the obstacles they face, and the assistance that comes to them from many sources, are the subject of this book.

People who migrate across borders are usually seen as occupying two different spheres: labor migrants are associated with voluntary migration and economic motives and behavior; refugees are associated with forced migration, traumatized responses, and dependency on relief assistance. Until recently, the social sciences treated the two categories quite separately, but in recent years, this dichotomy has begun to be recast by scholars who seek to show that all migrants engage in a spectrum of behavior and motivation, and that it is often difficult to draw the boundaries clearly between forced and voluntary migration. Forcibly displaced people, such as refugees and internally displaced people, are beginning to be seen as economic actors too. Many of the innovative concepts and ideas influencing migration theory are being applied to the study of livelihood activities of refugees and their economic consequences for host communities, sending countries, and co-nationals in other countries. For example, the study of transnational livelihoods now includes refugees, and—for good or bad—terms like "irregular migrants" and "mobile livelihoods" (a term used to refer to circular migration between two countries) are also applied to refugees.

There is now a burgeoning literature on refugees in protracted situations, addressing issues like urbanization, conflict reduction, repatriation, gender inequity, and violence. But there are relatively few studies that probe deeply into how refugees pursue livelihoods. This book seeks to document and analyze their livelihood experiences by synthesizing recent work, particularly that of researchers such as Lacey Andrews, Shelley Dick, Sarah Dryden-Peterson, Cindy Horst, Loren Landau and Eric Werker. The book draws on their findings and the growing body of livelihoods research in humanitarian situations to gather what we know about the economic behavior and impact of refugee movements from a variety of social science perspectives. The book is intended for "non-experts," including undergraduate and graduate students taking courses or doing research on forced migration, as well as field practitioners and a general audience interested in refugee issues.

I wish to thank the following people for their support and input during the course of writing this book: Loren Landau, my frequent co-author, who proves that collaboration can be a rewarding experience; my research assistants Sarah Titus and

Christine Makori; my editor at Kumarian, Jim Lance; the faculty and staff of the Feinstein International Famine Center—who provide an institutional base that is more like a family than a work place; the partners and interns of the Alchemy Project; and the MIT Inter-University Migration seminar which has been a source of intellectual stimulus and learning for twenty years. Finally, I would like to acknowledge the friendship and support of Jill Kneerim, Bill Bell, and Kyra and Jean Montagu. I dedicate this book, with love and thanks for his patience, to my son, Sam McGuire.

Abbreviations and Acronyms

ARC	American Refugee Committee
AOR	affidavit of relationship
CMB	"cash money boys"
CORD	Christian Outreach for Relief and Development
CREDAP	Committee for Reflection on Agro-Pastoral Development
DLI	Development through Local Integration
DFID	Department for International Development
DP	displaced person
DRC	Democratic Republic of the Congo
ECRE	European Council on Refugees and Exiles
EPAU	Evaluation and Policy Analysis Unit
ERMA (Fund)	Emergency Refugee and Migration Assistance
EU	European Union
FINCA	Foundation for International Community Assistance
GF	Good Friends: Center for Peace, Human Rights and Refugees
IASFM (Conference)	International Association for the Study of Forced Migration
ICAR	Information Centre about Asylum and Refugees
IDP	internally displaced person
INAR	Instituto Nacional de Aopip aos Refugiados
IOM	International Organization for Migration
JVA	joint voluntary agency
LRA	Lords Resistance Army
M.A.L.D. (Thesis)	Master of Arts in Law and Diplomacy
MFI	microfinance institution
MMP	microfinance and microenterprise programme
MRA (account)	Migration and Refugee Assistance
NGOs	non-governmental organizations
OCHA	Office for the Coordination of Humanitarian Affairs
ODI	Overseas Development Institute
ORR	Office of Refugee Resettlement
ROSCAs	rotating savings and credit associations
SEEP (Network)	Small Enterprise Evaluation Project
SPLA	Sudan Peoples Liberation Army
SRS	Self-Reliance Strategy
UNDP	United Nations Development Programme

UNFPA	United Nations Population Fund (formerly United Nations Fund for Population Activities)
UNHCR	United Nations High Commissioner for Refugees
UNICEF	United Nations International Children's Emergency Fund
UNITA	União Nacional para a Independência Total de Angola (National Union for Total Independence of Angola)
UNRWA	United Nations Relief and Works Agency for Palestine Refugees in the Near East
USCR	United States Committee for Refugees
WFP	World Food Programme
WHO	World Health Organization
WIDER (Conference)	World Institute for Development Economics Research

Chapter 1
Introduction: Displaced Livelihoods

At the beginning of the twenty-first century, well over 30 million people have been displaced by conflict and violence in their home countries. A significant proportion of these—perhaps 20 million worldwide—remain internally displaced within their home country, some moving to safer villages nearby, others to urban areas.[1] Relatively few people have the resources to move far beyond their place of origin; in conflict zones, as in natural disasters, many people do not leave their homes at all, risking great danger and deprivation. Perhaps a third of those forcibly displaced by conflict and violence cross the border of their countries to seek safety and asylum in other countries, mostly in the developing world. By the end of 2003, according to the Office of the UN High Commissioner for Refugees (UNHCR), these refugees numbered some 9.7 million people, a decrease of about nine percent from the year before. Most did not travel much beyond the border zone of neighboring countries, staying close enough to monitor the situation at home, and preferring to be in a place somewhat familiar to them. Others traveled further, to the urban areas of host countries or, if they had the resources, onward to more distant destinations.

The popular image of refugees is that of a mass influx during an emergency: thousands of traumatized people pouring across a border and congregating in camps, where relief agencies try to meet their health and food needs. At this writing, December 2004, it is the emergency in Darfur, Sudan, that is in the news, but for every year of the past decade there were other sites: Liberians in 2003, Afghans in 2001, Kosovars in 1999, Rwandese in 1994. However powerful, these familiar images do not capture the reality of refugee life. For one thing, mass influxes of tens of thousands that occur over a short time are quite rare. Most forcibly displaced people move in small groups or as individuals, stopping to seek assistance en route and slipping across borders when they can, to join fellow refugee communities. Many refugees take up residence in camps under the care of various authorities, but a much greater number live among the local community, in rural or urban areas, and never register or seek international assistance. Common to almost all refugees, however, is the destitution that results from their flight experience, paired with a strong desire to support themselves by pursuing livelihoods. The ways in which they do this, the obstacles they face, and the assistance that comes to them from many sources, is the subject of this book.

A second reality of refugee situations, not captured by TV images, is the protracted nature of displacement. Once the emergency phase with its rush of aid and media attention has passed, many relief agencies depart—along with most of the

1

humanitarian assistance, which was aimed at meeting emergency needs. In most cases, however, the conflict in the refugees' home countries does not end with the emergency phase, and for thousands of refugees, return is not an imminent possibility. The mass repatriation of Albanian Kosovars from Macedonia and Albania that took place a scant six weeks or so after they were displaced from Kosovo in 1999 was an exception. In most cases—for Afghans, Congolese, Somalis, Liberians, Burmese, Sudanese, and many other nationalities—some repatriation occurs, but new outbreaks of violence and conflict arise, and refugees traverse the border, unable to return to live securely in their homelands. If mass repatriation does occur, there are always many who remain behind, unable or unwilling to return. Perhaps their homes have been destroyed or occupied by others; some are too traumatized by the events they have witnessed or experienced in their home countries; others continue to fear persecution if they return.

Most refugees remain in their country of first asylum for years as the civil strife and insecurity in their home countries plays out. For most there is little likelihood either of their being invited to become citizens of the asylum country or being resettled in a third country. Stuck in this limbo, refugees are in what is known as *protracted situations*. According to UNHCR:

> Using a crude measure of refugee populations of 25,000 persons or more who have been in exile for five or more years in developing countries, and excluding Palestinian refugees who fall under the mandate of UNRWA, it is estimated that, at the end of 2003, there were 38 different protracted situations in the world, accounting for some 6.2 million refugees in total. The great majority of such situations were to be found in Africa (not including North Africa), which comprised 22 major protracted refugee situations including 2.3 million refugees. However, in terms of numbers, the majority of refugees in protracted situations were located in the region covering Central Asia, Southwest Asia, North Africa and the Middle East..., where eight major protracted situations accounted for 2.7 million refugees. [The rest of] Asia comprised five major protracted refugee situations including 670,000 refugees, whereas the three major protracted situations in Europe accounted for 530,000 refugees.[2]

Whether in camps or self-settled among the local population, the living circumstances of refugees in protracted situations are economically challenging and unsafe, with few means to support or educate themselves and their children. They face security problems ranging from harassment by the authorities to crime and forced military recruitment. Refugees living in the border zones of host countries frequently suffer from the spillover of conflict from the home country and must pursue livelihoods in undeveloped and isolated areas, where both displaced and local people struggle to support themselves with few resources and many challenges.

One of the most daunting problems facing refugees in protracted situations is the decline in the level and quality of humanitarian assistance that occurs once the emergency phase has passed. In camps, this decline can be gradual and intermittent or quite sudden. For self-settled refugees not living in camps, there are almost no official sources of assistance, and they must rely on the good will of their hosts. In these circumstances, the resilience and creativity of the refugees are revealed in a wide range of survival strategies. Though faced with economic deprivation and marginalization, many refugees maintain their cultural practices and values, join and form communities, and meet all manner of livelihood challenges in new and familiar ways. How refugees do this—how they adapt their survival strategies and develop new ones to maximize all available resources and opportunities, and the obstacles they face in doing so—is explored in this book.

In exploring refugees' survival strategies and the obstacles they face, we are drawn into the political economy of war and displacement, and the global politics of asylum in the twenty-first century. Refugees are a subset of all international migrants, who numbered some 200 million in 2004.[3] While migrants share many similar livelihood experiences, the difference for refugees is the existence of a well-established international refugee regime led by the United Nations High Commissioner for Refugees (UNHCR), whose office, since 1950, has been mandated by UN member states to provide refugees with protection and assistance. Refugees offer us an opportunity to see how this humanitarian system acts as a direct source of livelihood support, and creates—albeit inadvertently—a set of obstacles arising from poorly designed programs and policies. The book ends with a discussion of ways in which international refugee assistance could better support livelihoods, and proposes a model for refugee policy that takes into account the political factors influencing host countries' responses to refugees in the twenty-first century. This book moves between a local and a global perspective. We examine the day-to-day activities of refugees as they pursue livelihoods in their communities, and we consider the role of the international organizations and states that assist or obstruct those same livelihoods.

The remainder of this chapter sets out some definitions used in this book and the economic rights of refugees prescribed in international refugee law. Chapters Two and Three explore the main sites—refugee camps and urban areas—where long-term refugees live and pursue livelihoods in host countries. These chapters describe how markets emerge, and the economic impact of refugees' activities both on the host community and the wider region. In Chapter Four, our perspective widens to explore the economic activities of refugees who leave their first countries of asylum and travel to third countries, either through resettlement or as asylum-seekers. This chapter explores the economic experience of refugees in third countries, and particularly how their links with their home countries affect their ability to pursue livelihoods and emerge from poverty. Chapter Five explores the role of the international refugee regime—international humanitarian organizations, nongovernmental relief agencies, donor countries and host governments—in supporting or obstructing the livelihood strategies of refugees. Can humanitarian assistance go beyond food aid and emergency services to support refugee livelihoods? We explore whether microfinance services and income generating programs offer realistic alternatives to traditional forms of humanitarian assistance, which usually come in the form of relief grants. Chapter Six concludes by considering alternative approaches to supporting the livelihoods of refugees in protracted situations. We consider how refugee assistance programs can be designed so as also to help host populations who are often as poorly off as the refugees, and who face their own economic and security problems. In many host countries, humanitarian services for refugees exist in parallel to a separate, underfunded set of services for the surrounding population. Refugees and nationals live apart, with separate systems for food and nutrition, education, health, and water and sanitation. As in all cases where such separation exists, the systems are far from equal, and often the balance tilts in favor of the refugees when it comes to meeting basic needs. On the other hand, when it comes to economic activities like trade or employment or working the land, it is the refugees who are at the disadvantage. Parallel and unequal systems represent a waste of resources, and an unfair and politically untenable distribution of supplies. This closing chapter proposes a model of refugee assistance that could improve the lot of both refugees and host populations. The model takes into account the current political climate of growing restrictions on refugees. The feasibility of the model is discussed, in light of refugee assistance policies in host countries that come closest to the model's approach. We end with a look at the kinds of advocacy strategies that could move institutions in these desirable directions. Ending this book with such a proposed model is intended to offer a challenge and stimulate debate on how to take the problem of refugee assistance forward.

Who Are Refugees and Asylum-Seekers?

In common parlance, refugees are people displaced by persecution, war, or conflict, who have fled across an international border and are in need of international humanitarian assistance. However, underlying this common usage of the word, is specific legal status associated with a complex and longstanding set of legal requirements and based on a definition set out in international agreements and refugee law.[4] Once states have ratified these international agreements—which most have by 2004—the act of conferring formal refugee status on a person includes assigning to him or her a set of rights and protocols, including protection and access to international humanitarian assistance. This gives those with formal refugee status a privileged position vis à vis other immigrants, and it is a status that is not quickly and easily conferred by states. Crossing a border in flight from danger is not sufficient to acquire it. People who have just fled across a border are technically *asylum-seekers*; in order to acquire refugee status they must first be assigned the status by the state. There are two ways in which this assignment is made: on an individual basis and as part of a group determination. The individual determination procedure requires that a person prove to the state that their experience of persecution warrants refugee status according to the definition set out in the 1951 Convention. Those who undergo this lengthy determination procedure and receive formal refugee status are referred to as "Convention refugees."[5] However, when a host country is confronted with many thousands of refugees from the same country, the procedures for conferring refugee status on an individual basis are too cumbersome, and an alternative mechanism has been devised which is known as group determination of status on a *prima facie* basis.[6] According to Bonaventure Rutinwa, group determination means the state recognizes those in a mass influx as refugees based on "the readily apparent, objective circumstances in the country of origin giving rise to exodus." The purpose of this group mechanism is "to ensure admission to safety, protection from refoulement [forced repatriation], and basic humanitarian treatment to those patently in need of it."[7] Most of the world's refugees have *prima facie* status. In 2003, some 64% of the world's 9.7 million refugees were granted refugee status on a group or *prima facie* basis, and less that a quarter (24%) were granted refugee status following individual determination.[8]

Prima facie refugee status is a presumptive status, that is, it presumes that the people granted refugee status would be defined as refugees if they underwent individual determination; and therefore, that they should be treated as refugees and entitled to all the rights of refugees, as stipulated by the 1951 Convention and other applicable instruments. However, while this mechanism is convenient in mass influx situations, it leads to several problems, which will be revisited later in this book. One is the difficulty of excluding criminals and combatants or other elements that are not deserving of international protection.[9] When these elements create problems for the host country, all the refugees suffer the consequences. In this book, for the sake of convenience, all people crossing the border from conflict-affected countries are referred to as refugees, regardless of their assigned legal status in the host country.

Some Characteristics of Protracted Refugee Situations

Cross-Border Movements

The picture of an acute mass influx, in which thousands of refugees cross the border in a short space of time, describes relatively few refugee situations. Most refugees travel as individuals or in small groups, leaving when they are able and often in secrecy; their movements constituting many trickles back and forth across borders over extended periods of time—depending on the ebb and flow of conflict in their home country. There are periods of increased refugee movement, but many countries never experience a mass influx; instead, refugee populations accumulate over prolonged periods, with return movements frequently interspersed. The situation of Liberian refugees in Côte d'Ivoire, described by Tom Kuhlman is illustrative:

> By the end of 1990, the Liberian refugee caseload in Côte d'Ivoire had increased to 272,000. In succeeding years, the numbers rose and fell as the civil war worsened or abated. The maximum may have been as high as 400,000 in the mid-1990s....From 1996 onwards, many refugees returned home, well before UNHCR began its organized repatriation

programme in 1997; by the end of 2000, 70,500 refugees had been repatriated with UNHCR assistance, but more had left of their own accord. Even as the repatriation was underway, the violence in Monrovia in 1998 provoked a new wave of 23,000 refugees towards Côte d'Ivoire.[10]

This movement back and forth across the border is characteristic of protracted refugee situations, and as we shall see, has important implications for refugees' economic activities.

Patterns of Settlement

Once across a border, refugees are in the country of first asylum, or the host country, and their first task is to find accommodation. An important decision is where and how to live. A significant proportion of refugees stay away from camps or official settlement sites, and settle themselves among the local population—in rural hamlets and small towns, in "refugee villages," near towns, or in the shanty towns of megacities. This pattern is known as self-settlement or dispersed settlement. Many do not register with the authorities, and thus are without legal status. Generally, self-settled refugees do not receive official government or international assistance, relying instead on the hospitality of the host community. They share local households or set up temporary accommodation, and are helped with shelter and food by their own networks or by community or religious organizations. According to Sarah Dryden Peterson and Lucy Hovil,

> While "official" refugees fall under the control of the national government structures… self-settled refugees tend to operate within the local government structures, both rural and urban. They are integrated into their host community, pay graduated tax, contribute to the local economy, and even run in local council elections. However, their legal status remains insecure and ambiguous: they fall within the category of *prima facie* refugees, but are in danger of being seen as illegal immigrants.[11]

In some host countries, self-settled refugees are left undisturbed, but when there are very large numbers—or mass influxes—host governments often restrict refugees to areas near the border, usually in camps or settlements of some kind. This policy is based on various concerns, including security, manageability of large numbers, and the desire to prevent refugees from moving to the urban areas. In some cases, refugees themselves prefer to live in camps, since there they have access to humanitarian resources, including the possibility of resettlement. We will return to these issues in later chapters.

As shown in Table 1.1, of the 14.6 million persons of concern to UNHCR in 2001, some 60 percent were self-settled—13 percent (1.9m) in urban areas, and 47 percent (6.9m) dispersed in rural areas (or their type of settlement was unknown)—the other 40 percent (5.8m) resided in camps. In Africa and Asia, more than 50 percent of refugees live in camps and ten percent live in urban areas.[12] However, we should be cautious about these statistics. Refugees' often desire to remain

Table 1.1: Location of Officially Recognized Refugees

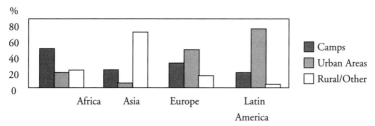

Source: Figures from UNHCR Statistics Unit. Chart adapted from *Alchemy Project Annual Report, 2003* (famine.tufts.edu/work/refugees.html).

flexible about their living arrangement, and this means they can be unwilling to be counted and reluctant to reveal their exact locations to authorities. The numbers and proportions of refugees in different types of settlements are notoriously difficult to determine, although it is generally accepted that the number of self-settled refugees is much higher than that of refugees living in camps.[13]

Whether refugees choose to self-settle in urban or rural areas, or to live with humanitarian assistance in camps and official settlements, will affect their economic experience in the host country. However, as we discuss in Chapter Two, settlement is a fluid process, depending on when refugees arrived, their survival strategies, the local socioeconomic and security conditions, and the actions of local and national authorities. Earlier arrivals may settle in different situations than later ones. Self-settled refugees can be forcibly relocated into camps by local authorities, and sometimes refugees move out of camps and become self-settled, or back into them. Many refugee households use camps as part of a broad strategy of survival: in which the workers live outside in order to farm or find employment, and the non-workers (elderly, mothers, and children) live in the camp where they have access to assistance. Refugees move in and out of the camps to find work, to trade, to explore repatriation options, to join the rebels, to visit, or to move to the city. They might return to the camps during the hungry season, or when there are security threats outside, or to use the camp schools. If camps are near towns, refugees living in the town pay social visits or come to the camp when resettlement interviews are being conducted. In turn, camp refugees go into towns to engage in various economic activities or to go to school. Local people frequent the camps too—making use of schools and health clinics set up by aid agencies, buying and selling in camp markets, or sometimes posing as refugees in order to get food aid. Refugees living in camps are never fully separated from the local community because of the difficulty of preventing movement in and out by both refugees and local people. Many host areas have a history of migration and mingling with the people who are now refugees. For example, in north-western Tanzania, the town of Kigoma on the shore of Lake Tanganyika has long been a migration target for Congolese on the other side of the lake, and Congolese and Tanzanians have historically mixed together for purposes of trade, marriage, entertainment, and seasonal work. This fluidity has strong implications for the constraints and opportunities for refugees' economic activities and their impact on the host community.

Why Refugees Do Not Go Home

In most protracted situations—where refugees have lived in host countries for at least three years (and often many more)—refugees cannot go home because the war, conflict, or persecution of ethnic groups in their home countries is not over, and it is unsafe for them to return. This is presently the case for refugees from Liberia, the Democratic Republic of the Congo (DRC), Burundi, Mauritania, Algeria, Sudan, Burma, Colombia, and others. What about situations where the war is over, where peace accords have been signed, and perhaps even where the government calls for refugees to return? This is currently the case in Rwanda, Angola, Sierra Leone, and—to some extent—in Afghanistan (although the conflict is not over), Bosnia, and Eritrea, among others. There are two linked reasons why long-term refugees do not return in these situations. One is that individuals still do not consider it safe, either for their particular ethnic group, or for the region of the country to which they would return. Peace is seldom spread homogenously across post-conflict countries,[14] and there are often pockets of resistance or ongoing conflict, which pose dangers to returnees. It is not uncommon for conflict to break out in parts of the country, as the peace is consolidated. This has occurred in Liberia repeatedly, and in Angola, Sierra Leone, eastern Congo, southern Sudan and Afghanistan. Many refugees adopt a "wait and see" attitude, and remain in their host countries—sometimes for several years—after peace accords are signed. As part of their repatriation programs, UNHCR sets up "go and see" visits, in which refugees are taken on visits to their home areas, to see and appraise the situation for themselves, then come back and report to others in the camp. If their judgment of the situation is negative, this will be communicated to others, quickly dampening prospects for return. Shelly Dick quotes a Liberian refugee living in Ghana in 2000:

> I would like to go back [to Liberia] some day, but not while Taylor is in power. I have friends who went back in 1995. Then the war came again in 1996 and things were much worse for them than the first time they ran. They had to run back to Ghana for a second time. They said going back to Liberia was the worst mistake they ever made. How can you go back to that kind of insecurity?[15]

Refugees' concerns about safe return are usually shared by relief agencies. In recent years, repatriation programs insisted upon by host governments—to countries like Burundi, Liberia, southern Sudan, and Afghanistan—have been strongly disputed by some agencies.

A second reason why refugees do not return, even where peace agreements have held and security is not a major concern, is because economic conditions in home countries devastated by years of conflict make the reconstruction of livelihoods very difficult. Roads and other transportation infrastructure are destroyed, and access to land is prevented by leftover problems from the war, such as mines or unexploded ordinance. At the village level, displacement and loss of life means social networks are disrupted or destroyed. In addition, most returnees lack the financial capital needed to re-establish their businesses or farms in their home countries. Given these problems, it is difficult for returnees to restart their livelihoods, and refugees often delay their return journey—preferring to wait until they can gather sufficient resources to ensure that they can put together a life when they return.

There are other reasons why refugees in protracted situations delay returning home. For some, it is the prospect of overwhelming family obligations in the home country. One Liberian refugee at Buduburam camp in Ghana, said,

"I stay here because if I go home there are many people to take care of. My sister and brother have many children and they will ask me to help them. They think that because I am in Ghana I have more money to help. I want to help them but how can I? In Liberia you can work for two weeks or a month and when you go to collect your pay there is no money."[16]

For others, the lives they have constructed during their exile—even if they have been in a refugee camp—are better than the ones to which they would return in their home country. Even in camps, most refugees are fairly safe, with access to schools and health facilities, and some opportunities to pursue livelihoods—none of which is guaranteed in their home country. Some refugees remain in camps and hold onto their refuge status, so that they can remain eligible for resettlement in third countries like the United States or Europe. Last, and by no means least, many refugees have very bad memories of their homeland: including the loss of relatives and their own devastating ordeals of flight—any of these are enough to make refugees unwilling to ever return.

Refugees with prima facie status often find themselves in a precarious legal position when the civil war or conflict in their home country ends. Although UNHCR stipulates that all returns should be voluntary, the situation depends on the host government's position. In some countries, the government decides that refugees should return, and requires that those wishing to remain in the host country regularize their immigration papers, and either qualify as Convention refugees (prove their eligibility as individual refugees rather than prima facie ones) or risk being deported.[17] In host countries that are slow to execute determination procedures or other immigration requirements, long-term refugees usually continue living as de facto refugees— hoping the government will leave them alone—but in aprecarious legal situation.

Refugee Livelihoods

The study of refugee livelihoods is part of the body of research on livelihoods in zones of prolonged conflict and instability.[18] There are multiple strands of this research: including frameworks for understanding the context,[19] policy analysis regarding humanitarian assistance,[20] anthropological accounts of conflict-affected diasporas and their networks,[21] and the role of humanitarian assistance—both in supporting conflict reduction and peace capacities,[22] and in contributing to the conflict.[23] Much of this livelihoods research is useful for analyzing and understanding the economic experience of refugees, and there is now a growing body of research on "displaced livelihoods"—the experience of forced migrants and the role of migration in livelihoods.[24]

The economic impact of conflict and displacement on a household can be understood using an assets framework. Each household has a portfolio of assets, or types of capital, which are the things it needs, uses, and has access to, in order to pursue livelihoods.[25] Assets include different types of capital:

- Natural capital (land, water, forests);
- Physical capital (livestock, equipment, infrastructure like roads, buildings);
- Human capital (education and skills, life experience, health);
- Social capital (community trust and knowledge, networks);
- Financial capital (stocks and flows) which include:
  ○ Regular inflows of money through earned income, state transfers (for example pensions), and remittances;
  ○ Savings, in the form of cash, bank deposits, or liquid assets like livestock and jewelry; and
  ○ Credit, including access to credit institutions.

In conflict zones—like southern Sudan, eastern Congo, Afghanistan, and Burma—from which people are eventually displaced, all forms of household capital are seriously compromised. Assets are stolen or destroyed ("stripped"), and access to them is blocked or endangered. Physical assets like cattle, harvests, or transportation equipment is stolen or destroyed, both by raiding militias and as a result of a widespread instability, increased crime, and breakdown of law and order. Access to physical and natural capital like street markets, businesses, farms, or grazing land, is reduced because of the dangers associated with travel. People on the roads risk being caught in the crossfire between armed groups and encounters with armed roadblocks or roving gangs of bandits. Mines are a particular danger and threat to livelihoods; they are often laid in random or unanticipated ways, including in roads and fields. The dangers of travel mean reduced contact with markets and vendors, and decreased circulation of goods, services, and money. Availability of and access to social services—such as health or education—is also reduced, as personnel flee and sites come under attack. For example, in the northeastern Congo, near Bunia, it is common for hospitals to be assailed because they treat both sides of the ethnic conflict.

When people flee their homes in conflict zones, they have often lost everything that enables them to earn their own living. Whether they become internally displaced or cross the border to become refugees, they use up their last resources to finance the journeys. For example, most Afghan refugees who came to Pakistan during the late 1990s had been internally displaced in Afghanistan for months, as a result of both drought and the conflict. Many had been impoverished by the need to give the Taliban cash to avoid being forcibly recruited, or by damage to their property or livelihoods through war, leaving no resources with which to survive the current severe drought. They arrived impoverished, having had to sell everything they had left to pay for the journey to Pakistan.[26]

The constraints and challenges facing refugees are similar to those of all people, whether displaced or not, trying to survive in conflict zones. Their economic activities tend to be based in the informal sector, oriented towards generating quick cash, and characterized by low financial risk.[27] The following kinds of cash-generating activities are common:

- Buying and selling goods like firewood, charcoal, vegetables, prepared food, cigarettes, and sweets, on a daily basis (hawking);
- Services provided by hair dressers/beauticians, mechanics, food preparation, construction, telephone booths (where individual calls on a cell phone are sold), and courier services (including carrying money and other goods between town and villages);
- Special services by and for refugees like language tutoring or interpreting.

Income level depends on whether a person owns the small business or works for the owner, and on the cost of the credit needed to jumpstart the business. These activities generate small, irregular sums of money—which for many are insufficient and must be supplemented by other kinds of work—sometimes including high-risk activities, like prostitution or smuggling. In conflict zones where there is also commercial resource extraction (legal or illegal), like mining, logging, or oil extraction, many people also derive livelihoods from these industries.

In our livelihoods research conducted during the course of the Alchemy Project,[28] almost all of the economically active refugees with whom we worked were engaged in informal, sector-based, small enterprises of some kind—often supplemented with wage work, such as part-time employment with aid agencies (as teachers or translators or program staff). In camps, most refugees obtained some income by selling food rations (often the only source of cash income) or with "piecework" on local farms or households when the opportunity arose. Many tried to start a small business with cash left over after household needs were met, but for most, this amount was insufficient to start a sustainable business without a supplementary loan. In camps where cultivable land was available or could be negotiated from the local community (usually by UNHCR), refugees engaged in agriculture on a small scale, sometimes harvesting enough to sell in local markets.

One of the most marked effects of forced displacement is the need to shift or diversify livelihoods. For most displaced people the only real income-earning possibility lies in petty trade. Most refugees have no access to farmland (or rangeland for pastoralists), and displaced people are obliged to become entrepreneurs, since any form of employment except odd jobs is usually hard to find. Very few refugees find formal wage employment, and those who do find it mainly with aid agencies. In urban areas and refugee camps, few of those with professional skills like nursing or teaching are able to utilize them, despite the need for these occupations in many host countries. The move toward non-farm activities like trading is very important, especially for women.[29] Displaced pastoralists, deprived of their cattle and range-land by conflict, and settled in camps or villages, turn to other sources of income, like fishing or dairies. For example, in southern Sudan, displaced pastoralists like the Mundari people have discovered that the plentiful fish in the lakes and rivers can provide a livelihood. The Mundari traditionally had a disdain for fish as a food and for anyone who worked with fish, but the loss of their herds and the realization that fish is an important commodity have encouraged many to take up fishing as a liveli-hood.[30] In northeastern Kenya, displaced Somali pastoralists who have settled near the town of Wajir have started in the dairy business, and cooperatives of women sell milk in roadside stalls.[31] Urban migration by refugees is also a livelihood response, but refugees in urban areas face many occupational difficulties, which are magnified by their lack of legal status and the absence of much official assistance. We will return to this discussion in Chapter Three.

The Need for Cash and Credit

The losses and dislocations from conflict and the ensuing displacement mean that one of the most serious needs for displaced people is access to cash and credit. Cash can only be obtained by engaging in economic activities, but cash or credit is needed in order to jumpstart these activities. Refugees also need cash for other purposes: to meet basic needs, to pay for transportation to the capital to keep their papers in order, and to pay their debts before they can begin reconstructing their livelihoods. In refugee camps, many basic needs are met through relief programs, but not all are, and not usually for as long as the refugees need them. For example, in many camps, firewood for cooking is not provided as part of the ration, and refugees must either buy it from local vendors (for which they need cash), or leave the camp to find it in the bush, often quite a risky venture. For refugees not living in camps, both basic needs and the means to restart one's livelihood require cash or credit.

There are few sources of credit for refugees. In most host countries, refugees do not have access to savings and loans facilities of formal banks and credit institutions, and without bank accounts they lack both credit and a safe place to keep savings. One of the biggest problems faced by displaced people trying to save money is the insecure environment and lack of safe facilities, especially in urban areas. Refugees can borrow money from moneylenders, but their rates are very high. Displaced peo-ple must establish access to new sources of financial capital, either through tapping into home community networks that become re-established in new places, or by trying to access local credit networks and community banks. Community-based rotating savings and credit associations (ROSCAs) can be established in refugee camps, but these groups often require that members be solvent or have a source of income before they can join. Perhaps the most fortunate refugees in first asylum countries are those with family in other countries, especially the West, who send remittances. For those lucky few, remittances are a lifesaving source of income, but for those refugees in third countries who must send them, this obligation can be a serious drain on their income. We return to these issues in later chapters. First, we consider the context in which refugees pursue livelihood strategies.

The Institutional Context of Displaced Livelihoods

The ability of refugees in protracted situations to pursue livelihoods is both constrained and enabled by social, political, and institutional factors at the global, national, and local levels. At the global level, there are the *rights*—especially social and economic rights—assigned to refugees by international laws and agreements, plus the international expectation that refugees should receive humanitarian aid, protection, and advocacy from international organizations like UNHCR and nongovernmental organizations. At the national level, there is the *host government's policy* towards refugees, which may or may not be in line with the government's international obligations. At the local level, there is the host community in which refugees settle, which brings with it many factors affecting refugee livelihoods— including the response of the local authorities, local security, economic problems, and the attitudes of the local population. Here we briefly consider each of these components, and then explore them in more detail in the next two chapters, as they play out in camp and urban settings.

The Rights of Refugees to Engage in Economic Activities

The economic rights of refugees to pursue livelihoods are clearly set forth in the principle international instrument pertaining to refugees, the United Nations Convention Relating to the Status of Refugees, adopted in Geneva on 28 July 1951, and commonly referred to as the 1951 Convention (see Appendix A for the full text).[32] According to Articles 17 and 18 (Wage-Earning Employment and Self-Employment), the Contracting State shall accord to refugees lawfully staying in their territory:

> "the most favourable treatment accorded to nationals of a foreign country in the same circumstances, as regards the right to engage in wage-earning employment."

and

> "...treatment as favourable as possible and, in any event, not less favourable than that accorded to aliens generally in the same circumstances, as regards the right to engage on his own account in agriculture,

industry, handicrafts, and commerce, and to establish commercial and industrial companies.

In addition, the Convention requires that Contracting States give refugees the right to:

- Practice a liberal profession (Article 19);
- Choose their place of residence to move freely within its territory (Article 26);
- Obtain travel documents for the purpose of travel outside their territory (Article 28).

Other rights relating to refugees' economic activities include the imposition of taxes: Contracting States should "not impose upon refugees duties, charges, or taxes, of any description whatsoever, *other or higher than those which are or may be levied on their nationals* in similar situations." (Article 29, emphasis added). But the Convention does not forbid imposing fees or "charges in respect of the issue to aliens of administrative documents including identity papers." Refugees should also be permitted to "transfer assets which they have brought into its territory, to another country where they have been admitted for the purposes of resettlement" (Article 30). In general, the Convention requires that the Contracting States "shall as far as possible facilitate the assimilation and naturalization of refugees" (Article 34).

In addition to these rights, refugees are entitled to humanitarian assistance, but as discussed earlier, this assistance declines precipitously in protracted situations. Funding that is available during emergencies is cut off after a period of time, and soon only food rations for the most vulnerable are available, and even those eventually cease.[33] The reasons for cuts in the level of humanitarian assistance are both budgetary and substantive. UNHCR often has difficulty allocating funds to protracted situations, because most donors want humanitarian assistance directed at emergencies. But in addition, UNHCR and the host government sometimes use reduced rations to discourage the long-term presence of refugees and encourage repatriation. Whatever the reason, the lack of adequate assistance has significant implications for how refugees survive. The reluctance of donors to continue funding once the emergency phase has ended means UNHCR must triage its funding of long-term refugee situations. For every refugee situation, the level of assistance depends on the willingness and size of donor states' contributions. Low levels of funding require UNHCR to come up with alternative ways to support refugees, usually by encouraging self-sufficiency or self-reliance. We will return to this issue in Chapter Five.

Host Government Policy Regarding Refugees' Economic Activities

The economic rights assigned refugees by the 1951 Convention are clear, but to be effective they need to be implemented by host governments, and this implementation often fails to take place.

Every host country has (or is supposed to have, according to international refugee law) national refugee legislation, which sets out the country's official response to refugee arrivals and the conditions of their stay, including their freedom of movement and right to work. In many host countries, the rights of refugees to be economically active are ignored or overruled, or at best practiced irregularly. It is increasingly common for host governments to restrict all kinds of economic activities by refugees outside designated camp areas, in an effort to discourage permanence and encourage repatriation. If legislation does not exist, host governments usually issue regulations concerning where refugees should live, and their freedom to move around, seek work, and access social services. In recent years, an increasingly restrictive climate has prevailed in many key host countries.

A key problem in developing countries is that many host countries do not have specific laws pertaining to refugees, nor a clearly articulated refugee policy. When there is such a policy it is often unevenly or irregularly implemented, and some host countries, like Kenya, leave all refugee matters to UNHCR. In most countries, there are regulations on refugees' economic activities, usually restricting them to designated zones, or to areas within a designated distance of the camps. When these zones are in isolated areas, refugees have difficulty establishing livelihoods, particularly because of the resources they need to travel to markets to trade their goods.

Two of the main reasons for host governments' resistance to refugees' economic activities are security problems and resource burdens. During the 1980s, many host governments—particularly in Africa—cited the limited capacity of their national economies to absorb refugees as the primary reason for their desire that refugees should be fully taken care of by aid agencies, rather than be allowed to support themselves. Since the 1990s, security concerns have added an equally powerful reason to keep refugees segregated from the local community. Even when government policies are in place to assist refugees with economic activities, such as the Self-reliance Strategy in Uganda, security problems can overwhelm them. In northern Uganda, chronic violence and conflict between government forces and the rebel Lord's Resistance Army has severely disrupted the lives of both long-term Sudanese refugees living there and the local population. In Adjumani, for example, many refugees had become self-sufficient in terms of food production, but the upheavals from attacks and violence have caused refugees to flee their fields, and become once again dependent on direct assistance.[34] Faced with domestic economic problems of unemployment and poverty, together with security threats, few host governments are willing to be generous to refugees, preferring to keep them in camps where international relief agencies can take care of them and ensure they return to their home countries as soon as possible. That return is unlikely to occur soon nevertheless does not incline them to allow refugees their rights to economic freedom.

The Local Response: The Relationship Between the Local Population and the Refugees

A third factor affecting the context for refugee livelihoods is the host community and its local authorities. Many refugee-hosting areas are in remote locations, at a distance from the national capital, and the reach of the central government into these areas is weak, so it is often local or provincial authorities that decide how strictly to implement national policy. As outsiders and "guests," the ability of refugees to work and move around freely outside of camps is contingent upon the good will and cooperation of most of the local population, their leaders, and the local authorities. In the absence of this good will, refugees encounter hostility, antagonism, and even threats, and the host community is more likely to call on the national government to clamp down on refugees. When the local community accepts refugees, they are better able to hide from authorities, face fewer security threats, and are more able to pursue livelihoods. In some host countries, official policies of encampment are undermined or subverted by local chiefs and villagers who collaborate in enabling refugees to settle in the community.[35] Refugees' ability to pursue livelihoods depends on who benefits and who loses from their presence, and on whether the interests of the most powerful actors are being sufficiently served, or at least not subverted. There are multiple actors, or stakeholders, in a host area—including wealthy farmers and businessmen, poor peasants, and local authorities, such as chiefs and village leaders—each with varying interests in refugees and different degrees of power to block or enable refugees' economic activities.

One of the key issues mediating the relationship between the host community and refugees is *access to land*. Where refugees live in camps or settlements, their access to farm land is usually negotiated by either the government or UNHCR, but refugees must also have access to the commons to obtain basic necessities like firewood or construction timber, or grass for grazing if they want to keep livestock. Where land is scarce, tensions occur. An example is the case of Nakivale Refugee Settlement in western Uganda, which began in 1960 in response to an influx of Batutsi refugees fleeing the Bahutu regime that had taken power in Rwanda. The land for the settlement was acquired from the local king by the colonial government in exchange for other land. The Nakivale land was close to the border with Rwanda and had a low population of nationals because of infestation with tsetse fly. Nakivale has since hosted a wide diversity of refugee nationalities, and, as land constraints have grown in Uganda, tensions between refugees and nationals over access to the land in the Nakivale area has become a critical issue.[36]

By contrast, when land is abundant, sufficient for people to grow their own food, and the settlement is far from insecure borders, the situation is often calmer and less tense. Sarah Dryden Peterson contrasts the situation in Nakivale with that in Kyaka II Refugee Settlement in Kyenjojo District in western Uganda, where refugees live in harmony with locals and where everyone is able to grow their own food.[37] Similarly, in Zambia's western province, Angolan refugees have lived in peace for many years among Zambians, who regard them as hard workers, able to bring more land under production. This region of Zambia is relatively undeveloped and land—while not very fertile—is abundant. Most importantly, the locals do not perceive there to be security problems linked to the Angolans.

Security problems are serious obstacles to economic activity, making movement outside the camps dangerous, and affecting life inside the camps. On the part of the host community, initial sympathy and willingness to help the refugees often turns into resentment when they are perceived to create or aggravate security or economic problems. These threats and the resulting resentment increase when refugee numbers continue to grow or with new waves of arrivals. However, while security and resource burdens are real problems in many host areas, refugees are often blamed for pre-existing social or economic problems. Many host countries today are experiencing a range of rapid and disorienting economic, social, and political changes that have resulted in rises in crime and insecurity or declining standards of living. Such changes include the imposition of structural adjustment programs, proximity to conflict zones and/or involvement in the conflict, and public health crises like HIV-AIDS. In this context, refugees often become scapegoats and are more vulnerable and more likely to lack protection of their rights, including the right to work. This is illustrated in case of South Africa, currently struggling through a period of transition and stress as it recovers from the apartheid years. High levels of unemployment and a struggling economy, elevated crime rates, and widespread insecurity have led to harassment of migrants, among whom there are many urban self-settled refugees. In many host countries, local people believe that the presence of refugees is linked to the rise in criminal activity, delinquency, street prostitution, and drug proliferation. But many of these countries were already experiencing rising poverty, unemployment, and other structural economic problems that were not caused by refugees. While refugees can aggravate the social dislocations associated with this poverty, it is unlikely that they are responsible for them. The economic and social benefits to host communities of hosting refugees can outweigh the costs, particularly if policies are set up so as to take advantage of the refugees' presence.[38]

Notes

1   This book focuses on the experience of refugees, and does not address the larger problem of internally displaced people. Although the economic problems of IDPs are often similar to those of refugees, the policy context and politics of IDP situations are very different and will not be addressed in this book.

2   Executive Committee of the High Commissioner's Programme, "Protracted Refugee Situations" Standing Committee 30th Meeting, 10 June 2004; available at www.unhcr.ch.
      statistics. See also Jeff Crisp and Damtew Dessalegne, "Refugee Protection and Migration Management: The Challenge for UNHCR," (working paper, New Issues in Refugee Research, no. 64, UNHCR, 2002); Jeff Crisp "No Solutions in Sight: The Problem of Protracted Refugee Situations in Africa," (working paper, New Issues in Refugee Research, no. 75, UNHCR, 2002).

3   The official UN figure was 175 million international migrants in 2002, but some experts, including the Global Commission for International Migration,

think this is an undercount and think 200 million is a closer estimate (www.gcim.org).

4   The 1951 UN Convention defines a refugee as any person who: "owing to a well-founded fear of being persecuted for reasons of race, religion, nationality, membership of a particular social group or political opinion, is outside the country of his nationality and is unable or, owing to such fear or for reasons other than personal convenience, is unwilling to avail himself of the protection of that country." In 1969, the Organization of African States enlarged that definition for African states so as to include persons who: "owing to external aggression, occupation, foreign domination or events seriously disturbing public order in either part or the whole of his country of origin or nationality, is compelled to leave his place of habitual residence in order to seek refuge in another place outside his country…" For full definitions see Appendix A which contains the text of the 1951 Convention, and UNHCR's Web site: www.unhcr.ch.

5   Even those who have undergone full determination and have legal refugee status may find their actual rights and residence status to be insecure and incomplete. Not all host countries signatory to the Convention have implemented the Articles of the Convention. See Jennifer Hyndman and B.V. Nylund, "UNHCR and the Status of Prima Facie Refugees in Kenya," *International Journal of Refugee Law* 10(1/2) (1998): 21-48.

6   Bonaventure Rutinwa, "Prima Facie Status and Refugee Protection," (working paper, New Issues in Refugee Research, no. 69, UNHCR, 2002).

7   Rutinwa, "Prima Facie Status," 1.

8   UNHCR, "Global Refugee Trends: Overview of Refugee Populations, New Arrivals, Durable Solutions, Asylum-Seekers and Other Persons of Concern to UNHCR"; available at www.unhcr.ch/cgi-bin/texis/vtx/statistics.

9   See Rutinwa, "Prima Facie Status," 1.

10   Tom Kuhlman, *Responding to Protracted Refugee Situations: A Case Study of Liberian Refugees in Côte d'Ivoire*, report for UNHCR Evaluation and Policy Unit, 2002, 11.

11   Sarah Dryden-Peterson and Lucy Hovil, "Local Integration as a Durable Solution: Refugees, Host Populations and Education in Uganda," (working paper, New Issues in Refugee Research, no. 93, UNHCR, 2003), 6.

12   *UNHCR Statistical Handbook* 2001 (Geneva: UNHCR, 2001), 38; available at www.unhcr.ch/cgi-bin/texis/vtx/statistics.

13   See Bela Hovy, "Statistically Correct Asylum Data: Prospects and Limitations," (working paper, New Issues in Refugee Research, no. 37, UNHCR, 2001); and Jonathan Bascom, *Losing Place: Refugee Populations and Rural Transformations in East Africa* (New York: Berghahn Books, 1998), 26. For example in Uganda, at the end of 2002, the UNHCR reported a national

total of 197,082 refugees, primarily from Sudan, Democratic Republic of Congo (DRC), and Rwanda, who were registered with UNHCR and who living in settlement areas. However, according to Dryden-Peterson and Hovil (5) "In addition to this number, conservative estimates place the number of self-settled refugees in the country at approximately 50,000. In reality, the number is probably far higher. Furthermore, there are 10,000 refugees registered with the Office of the Prime Minister as self-sufficient urban refugees and it is estimated that 5,000 to 10,000 others live in Kampala without assistance or protection."

14 Rather than calling countries "post-conflict," a preferable term might be "post-peace accord" which describes the situation, but does not imply that conflict is over.

15 Shelly Dick, "Liberians in Ghana: Living without Humanitarian Assistance," (working paper, New Issues in Refugee Research, no. 57, UNHCR, 2002), 40.

16 Dick, "Liberians in Ghana," 49.

17 Dick, "Liberians in Ghana," 42.

18 G. M. Hamid, "Livelihood Patterns of Displaced Households in Greater Khartoum," *Disasters* 16 (1992): 230-239; Sue Lautze, E. Stites, N. Nojumi, and F. Najimi, "Qaht-E-Pool 'A Cash Famine': Food Insecurity in Afghanistan 1999-2002," (28 October 2002); available at famine.tufts.edu/pdf/cash_famine.pdf; Mark Vincent and Birgitte Sorensen, *Caught Between Borders: Response Strategies of the Internally Displaced* (London and Sterling, VA: Norwegian Refugee Council and Pluto Press, 2001); and T. Wilson, *Microfinance during and After Armed Conflict: Lessons from Angola, Cambodia, Mozambique and Rwanda* (Durham, UK: Concern Worldwide and Springfield Centre for Business in Development, 2002).

19 These include political analyses such as Joanna Macrae and Anthony Zwi eds. (with Mark Duffield and Hugo Slim), *War and Hunger: Rethinking International Responses to Complex Emergencies* (London: Zed Books in association with Save the Children Fund (UK), 1994); more policy-oriented frameworks such as DFID's Sustainable Livelihoods model (www.livelihoods.org), and the recent work that emphasizes the importance of vulnerability and risk and downplays the importance of sustainability in a livelihoods framework, for example Helen Young et al., *Nutrition and Livelihoods in Situations of Conflict and other Crises* (Medford, MA: Feinstein International Famine Center, Tufts University, 2002) and Adam Pain and Sue Lautze, *Livelihoods in Afghanistan* (Kabul: Afghanistan, Afghanistan Research and Evaluation Unit, 2002).

20 Recommendations concerning livelihood interventions in conflict and displaced situations include those concerned with providing shelter and access to productive assets as a means to support livelihoods, see S. Ellis

and S. Barakat, "From Relief to Development: The Long-Term Effects of 'Temporary' Accommodation of Refugees and Displaced Persons in the Republic of Croatia," *Disasters* 20 (1996): 111-124; R. Green, "Regaining and Securing Access to Common Property Resources," in *Risks and Reconstruction: Experiences of Resettlers and Refugees*, eds. Michael M. Cernea and Christopher McDowell (Washington, DC: World Bank, 2000), 253-290; and a very large literature on food security (for a review see Young et al., *Nutrition and Livelihoods*).

21   Many of these studies emphasize how different networks underpin and enable people's pursuit of livelihoods in conflict. See Janet MacGaffey and Remy Bazengguissa-Ganga, *Congo-Paris: Transnational Traders on the Margins of the Law* (Indiana: James Currey/Indiana University Press, 2000) for their study of Congolese traders in Paris, and Cindy Horst, "Vital Links in Social Security: Somali Refugees in the Dadaab Camps, Kenya," (working paper, New Issues in Refugee Research, no. 38, UNHCR, 2001) for her account of Somali networks.

22   This strand of research is exemplified in Mary Anderson's work and her Local Capacities for Peace Project which explores how humanitarian aid can help communities find and strengthen the peace capacities ("peace connectors") in their societies. See Mary B. Anderson, *Do No Harm; How Aid Can Support Peace-or War* (Boulder, CO: Lynne Rienner Publishers, Inc., 1999).

23   Marl Duffied, *Shifting Sands: The Search for 'Coherence' Between Political and Humanitarian Responses to Complex Emergencies,* Humanitarian Policy Group Report 8 (London: ODI, August 2001); D. Keen, "A Disaster for Whom? Local Interests and International Donors During Famine among the Dinka of Sudan," *Disasters* 15 (1991): 58-73; and J. Goodhand and D. Hulme, "Understanding Conflict and Peace-Building in the New World Disorder," *Third World Quarterly* Vol. 20(1) (1999): 13-26.

24   See for example, M. Cernea, "The Risks and Reconstruction Model for Resettling Displaced Populations," *World Development* 25 (1997): 1569-1587; A. De Haan, "Livelihoods and Poverty: The Role of Migration—A Critical Review of the Migration Literature," *The Journal of Development Studies* 36 (1999): 1-47; K. Ogden, "Coping Strategies Developed as a Result of Social Structure and Conflict: Kosovo in the 1990s," *Disasters* 24 (2000): 117-132; Dick, "Liberians in Ghana"; Karen Jacobsen, "Livelihoods in Conflict: The Pursuit of Livelihoods by Refugees and the Impact on the Human Security of Host Communities," (expert working paper, Center for Development Research Study: Migration-Development Links: Evidence and Options, February 2002).

25   This section draws on the discussion of this framework and the different types of capital in Pain and Lautze, *Livelihoods in Afghanistan*, 9-14. See also www.livelihoods.org/info/info_guidancesheets.html#11

26   U.S. Committee for Refugees (USCR), "Pakistan: Afghan Refugees Shunned and Scorned," (Washington, DC, September 2001); available at www .refugees.org/world/articles/pakistan_introduction_2001.htm.

27   Wilson, *Microfinance,* 1.

28   Karen Jacobsen, "Supporting Displaced Livelihoods with Microcredit and Other Income Generating Programs: Findings from the Alchemy Project, 2001-2004," Feinstein International Famine Center, Tufts University. November 2004; available at www.famine.tufts.edu

29   Grace Carswell, "Livelihood Diversification in Southern Ethiopia," (working paper, Institute of Development Studies, no. 117, 2000).

30   *Alchemy Project Annual Report 2002,* Alchemy Project, Feinstein International Famine Center, Tufts University, Medford, MA, 2002; available at famine.tufts.edu/index.html?id=18.

31   Maitri Morarji, *Alchemy Project Field Assessment: Arid Lands Development Focus, Wajir, Kenya,* Alchemy Project Country Report No. 6 (August 2004); available at www.famine.tufts.edu.

32   For a discussion of these rights, and several relevant articles, see USCRI, *World Refugee Survey,* 2004, (Washington, DC, 2004); available at www .refugees.org/wrs04/main.html

33   Shelly Dick (23-24) cites the case of Liberian refugees in Ghana: "By August 1996 when Liberia's civil war officially ended, Ghana was said to be providing asylum for an estimated 17,000 Liberians…Up to that point the humanitarian aid regime was in full operation providing food rations, education, health care and other basic needs for the refugees…as of 1997 assistance was greatly reduced. By 1998, the loan scheme was discontinued and food rations were only distributed to the most vulnerable refugees…As of 30 June 2000 even food rations for vulnerable refugees ceased and all humanitarian assistance…was withdrawn from Liberians according to UNHCR regional policy…"

34   As reported by Dryden-Peterson and Hovil (9), an extreme case of security threat was the Achol-Pii Refugee Settlement in Pader District, Uganda. In July 1996, the Lords Resistance Army (LRA) attacked the settlement killing over 100 unarmed refugees and wounding several others. After a passionate appeal to the government of Uganda to relocate them to the southern parts of the country, the Government responded that the refugees had no right to decide where to be housed and that if they were tired of government's hospitality, they should go back to their country of origin. Unable to return to Sudan, the majority remained in Achol-Pii. Despite numerous reports warning of an imminent attack on the settlement in 2002, the government did not act. On August 5, 2002, the LRA again attacked Achol-Pii Refugee Settlement killing more than 20 refugees, injuring several others, and displacing 23,000.

35   Oliver Bakewell, "Repatriation and Self-Settled Refugees in Zambia: Bring-ing Solutions to the Wrong Problems," *Journal of Refugee Studies* 13, no. 4 (2000): 370.

36   Dryden-Peterson and Hovil, "Local Integration," 13.

37   Dryden-Peterson and Hovil, "Local Integration," 17.

38   See, among others, Karen Jacobsen, "The Forgotten Solution: Local Integra-tion for Refugees in Developing Countries," (working paper, New Issues in Refugee Research, no. 45, UNHCR, 2001); Dryden-Peterson and Hovil, "Local Integration," 7; Tania Kaiser, *A Beneficiary-Based Evaluation of the UNHCR Programme in Guinea*, report for UNHCR Evaluation and Policy Analysis Unit, 2001; Crisp, "No Solutions"; Barbara Harrell-Bond, "Toward the Economic and Social 'Integration' of Refugee Populations in Host Coun-tries in Africa," (conference, Stanley Foundation, "Refugee Protection in Africa: How to Ensure Security and Development for Refugees and Hosts," Entebbe, Uganda, November 2002).

Chapter 2
Economic Survival in Refugee Camps

uch has now been written about refugee camps and their role in regional security and geopolitics, as well as in humanitarian politics. Camps have been analyzed for the dual role they play, both as refuges for the war-displaced and as sanctuaries for so-called "refugee-warriors". Camps are seen as security problems, political problems, humanitarian problems, and as factors in war economies.[1] The social experience of refugees who live for long periods in camps is increasingly well documented, largely by anthropologists and geographers. In this chapter, we focus on the economic experience of refugees who live for long periods in camps, and how they survive declining levels of humanitarian assistance. As refugee situations become protracted, the gradual or sometimes sudden reduction of humanitarian assistance, including food rations, becomes a serious problem in camps. The longer a protracted situation persists, the more likely it is that the overall budget for that program shrinks and assistance is repeatedly cut.[2] Protracted situations are often interspersed with periods of attempted repatriation, but unless peace is well established in the refugees' home country, renewed conflict leads to repeated outflows—often back to old camps that were closed after the attempted repatriation. The re-opened camps no longer benefit from the international attention and assistance that came with the press-attended first emergency. For example, after conflict increased in Afghanistan in 2000, tens of thousands of destitute Afghan refugees crossed into Pakistan and went to Jalozai, a former refugee camp that had been home to ethnic minority refugees during the 1990s. They found little aid there, and according to USCR, conditions at Jalozai were soon among the worst of any refugee camp in the world.[3]

With reduced aid, refugees must find ways to support themselves and their families by taking advantage of whatever economic resources are available in and outside of camps. All available resources—especially those provided by humanitarian aid agencies—are utilized, often in unexpected ways. Small-scale enterprises and informal sector activities—sometimes including illicit endeavors—are widespread. Most people sell or trade some portion of their food rations, and depending on available opportunities, refugees work outside the camps as farmers, gold miners, domestic help, camel butchers, musicians, and second hand clothes traders. They provide any number of informal services from cell phones to shoe making to truck repair to specialized hair braiding. A few lucky refugees have relatives abroad who send remittances. Military recruitment for boys and prostitution for girls and boys become survival strategies. Since refugees and locals are generally permitted to move in and out of camps, they are linked into the local and even regional economy, facilitated by the widespread use of mobile phones, trade, and sometimes commercial transporta-tion. For example, Kakuma camp, on the Kenya-Sudan border, is linked to Nairobi by a well-used bus service that makes the ten-hour trip on a weekly basis, even though refugees are not permitted to be in Nairobi. In some cases, this flow of goods and people goes further, to markets in the home country and to the diaspora abroad.

Host governments increasingly require refugees to live in camps, but they are often unable or unwilling to enforce such policies, and do little to prevent refugees from pursuing economic activities. National governments are not the only actors with interests in refugees' economic activities. Rebel groups, local authorities, employers, traders, and refugee leaders all seek to take advantage of the presence of refugees and the aid that accompanies them. This chapter explores how refugees negotiate the systems of control imposed by these actors in order to gain access to the resources they need to survive and even prosper. Over time, camps have local economic implications, both in terms of increased competition for resources and as a source of economic stimulus—particularly in isolated and remote border regions. This chapter describes the nature of camp economies, the kinds of economic activ-ities commonly found there, and the social and cultural factors that shape economic outcomes both for the refugees and for the wider host region. The chapter is struc-tured in terms of the refugees' economic experience, beginning with the initial flight across borders and arrival in camps, then examining the post-emergency or pro-tracted phase.

Flight and Arrival: An Economic Perspective

By the time they get to camps, most refugees are destitute and traumatized as a result of their flight across the border, or the period preceding their flight when they were internally displaced. People fleeing from conflict and violence often have to make hasty decisions about leaving and flee without bringing any assets with them. Those who do manage to carry money or other assets (such as livestock or bicycles or cars) with them are at an advantage, because during flight these can be used for bribes or to pay for transportation. For example, Congolese refugees who traverse Lake Tan-ganyika to get to Tanzania have to pay local fishermen extortionate fees to cross the lake. Assets are used up, lost, or stolen during the course of their journeys, and most refugees arrive in camps with little to help them start economic activities. Those few who manage to bring livestock, vehicles, or electronic equipment are at an advan-tage, but most arrive only with their labor power, skills, and experience. Other less tangible economic resources are also lost to a household during flight. Family mem-bers who played a key role in the household's economy may have been killed or sep-arated. Community networks are destroyed, reducing refugees' access to social capital. For many, the experience of flight is highly traumatic, and may include being raped or being witness to murder and other atrocities—often with members of their own families among the victims. Most refugees arrive in very serious emotional and physical condition, often wounded, ill, or malnourished. Bereft of their assets, they must begin their personal and economic recovery from a very low place. That so many do is a story of great courage and empowerment.

The Evolution of a Refugee Camp

Under these circumstances of need and loss, assistance is crucial for the survival of newly arrived refugees. During or soon after a mass influx, there is an influx of humanitarian assistance and resources in the form of food aid and services like health care, shelter, nutrition support, and trauma counseling, provided by many diverse NGOs and international organizations. In some emergencies, the western press also arrives, and scenes of refugee misery appear on TV screens, along with appeals for western audiences to help the refugees. This emergency phase lasts for several months, until many of the relief organizations depart, their work of stabilizing the health and nutritional problems done. (The press usually leaves long before the aid agencies do.) The "care and maintenance" phase ensues, in which a core of operational NGOs remains in the camps to provide food aid and basic services such as water, sanitation, and health services. Agricultural and income-generating programs are sometimes implemented as a way to encourage self-reliance in the face of reduced assistance. A "lead agency" usually coordinates these activities, with UNHCR providing oversight and advocating to the government on behalf of the refugees. A government official presides over the camp. As time passes, if the refugees do not return to their country of origin, or find other solutions such as resettlement or local integration, a protracted refugee situation develops and refugee camps become more permanent fixtures.

Camp Economies

The movement of goods and people in and out of camps makes it somewhat inaccurate to speak of a "camp economy" as though it was closed off from the surrounding region, however the experience of camp refugees is different enough from self-settled refugees living outside camps to justify examining their experiences separately. The key advantage for refugees living in camps is access to humanitarian assistance, and many refugee households have members living both inside and outside camps, in order to take advantage of both situations. Even when assistance decreases over time, camp refugees can incorporate these resources into their household income strategies, thereby increasing their ability to diversify risk and maximize income. The main constraints are the remoteness of camps and restrictions on refugees' freedom to engage in economic activities outside. We begin with a description of the main economic activities in camps, then review the constraints and enabling factors characterizing the economic activities of camp refugees.

Camp Markets

By far the most common camp activity is trade, conducted either in the camp market or in local town markets. Typically, a camp will have one or more markets where small businesses are concentrated[4] and where trade in locally produced and imported goods is conducted. Camp markets can be large, with many sectors. Almost everyone has something to trade, ranging from the poorer refugees who sell small amounts of food rations or vegetables they have grown or firewood collected outside the camp, to small entrepreneurs who are able to get credit and start a small trading business or service. Wealthier merchants whose clientele come from outside the camps trade in gold and diamonds, currency, and—in all likelihood—other items hidden from the view of visiting researchers. The range and diversity of economic activities in camp markets is illustrated in the following examples, taken from the author's field notes when she visited the camps during the period stated in parentheses:

- Ifo camp for Somali and other refugees, Dadaab, northeastern Kenya (July 1996). Somalis cross the border and locals come from all around to buy or sell in the camel market and butchery. Another section of the camp market contains coffee "hotels," a shaded section with small stools where Ethiopian refugees serve coffee in china cups from their home regions.
- Lugufu camp for Congolese refugees, near Kigoma, western Tanzania (July 2000). One block of the market is dominated by gold and diamond traders from the DR Congo who set up their tiny scales in stalls. Whether they are refugees or not was hard to tell, as they drifted away from their stalls and disappeared into the crowd as soon as they saw us approach. Another section was devoted to music, with an excellent selection of music cassettes from many African countries. Samples of the music played from speakers and the vendors danced in front of their stalls with anyone who wanted to join in.
- Site 2, the camp for Cambodian refugees during the 1980s-early 90s, Aranyaprathet, Thailand (February 1990). By now the camp is well established and the market is large with goods ranging from non-food rations to rubies smuggled across the border from the mountains in western Cambodia where they are mined. Well-swept streets are lined with shops and restaurants where we ate lunch every day, along with members of the aid agencies and many refugees. An efficient bicycle rickshaw taxi service ferries goods and people throughout the camp.
- Nangweshi camp for Angolan refugees, western Zambia (August 2004). The market is well organized, with a central section containing cement tables where refugees sell vegetables,

dried fish, candy, scones, small building materials, and charcoal. Surrounding this section are five alleys, each containing some twenty stalls specializing in the sale of items such as second hand clothes (from relief shipments), local cloth, and household wares. Slightly further away are one or two free-standing shops, supplied with electricity from a portable generator which allow patrons to enjoy Cape Verdean dance music played from a large ghetto blaster. The two shops we visited were filled with goods imported from Namibia and South Africa, including new clothes and shoes, electronic appliances and the batteries for them, all kinds of delicacies, and various things discreetly hidden under the counter. Everything was priced beyond the means of the refugees in the camp and was clearly intended for non-camp residents. The shopkeeper, a young, well dressed man, declined to be explicit about how he had been able to stock his shop, but later our refugee translator explained that most of the wealthier shopkeepers started off by selling smuggled diamonds from Angola.

Trade in Aid

Food aid is the most basic and ubiquitous form of humanitarian assistance. It is a huge global industry, controlled by the World Food Programme,[5] and is clearly also seen by refugees as an economic resource. Food rations and ration cards are widely sold to generate income, mainly by selling them in markets in or outside camps. Food items in the ration that are inappropriate to the refugees' cultural preferences are especially likely to be sold to locals in order to buy more desirable foodstuffs. For example, Liberians' staple food is rice, but, as Lacey Andrews describes, in Sembakounya camp in Guinea, for a time they received bulgur in the food ration:

> The white "Japanese" bulgur was well received for the month it was distributed as it looked like, had a similar texture, and chewed like rice. But "You haven't eaten if you haven't had rice" is a common saying, so it is no wonder that much of this highly-touted protein source of bulgur is sold off to buy rice and the condiments necessary to make a good sauce: pepper, tomato paste and tomatoes, potato and cassava leaves, garlic, dried fish, and for those with more money, perhaps vegetables like onions and potatoes and eggplant/jaxatu and even meat or chicken or fish or beans.[6]

While the sale of food aid is not using it as it was intended, it can support refugee livelihoods by providing a source of income. Aid agencies are well aware that food aid is not always matched to refugees' normal diets, and that refugees sell their food rations, and sometimes the agencies deliberately factor this practice into their calculations about refugee rations. The World Food Programme, however, usually tries to limit this practice, by controlling the distribution of food and ration cards.[7]

One indirect effect of having food aid as a livelihood resource is that it keeps refugees in the camps. When food aid is cut off, it can negatively affect refugees' health and their livelihoods, and can lead to new displacement as well as urban migration.

Non-food aid, such as clothes, household items, construction materials and so forth, are also traded. Refugees can sometimes get higher prices in local markets for "imported" aid items, and can then purchase the cheaper local goods and make a small profit. In Semabkouya camp in Guinea, "Refugee small businesses get their start at the market by selling non-food aid items, particularly pot sets and blankets, as well as food rations. A full pot set and plates can bring as much as 18,000 GF (Guinean francs). Replacement pots can be bought for as little as 9,000 GF, so this leaves a sufficient amount to invest in a new business (a kilo of rice is 600GF)."[8]

Trade in Services

All kinds of services are available in the camp. Many people sell cooked food, or keep restaurants and coffee shops. In large camps, cooked lunches for international aid personnel (and camp visitors) are a good source of income for refugees. Men and women engage in tailoring, carpentry, construction, radio repair, mechanics, hair dressing, and other beauty services. Wherever camps fall short of some basic need, a service pops up to supply it. For example, there is high demand for telephone service in camps, because refugees want to keep in touch with their relatives and networks abroad. In camps where reception is possible, refugees with cell phones set up calling booths and charge customers by the minute for calls made and received. These one-man enterprises can blossom into more complicated businesses. Shelly Dick writes that in Budumbara camp for Liberian refugees, near Accra, Ghana, the first communication centre at the camp, called BuduCom, was established in 1995, introducing cell phones for receiving calls.

> People paid a small registration fee, then when a call came in, a BuduCom employee took the phone by bicycle to the registered address of the person receiving the call. As of September 2000, there were ten communication centres at the camp, four owned by Liberians and six owned by Ghanaians who hire Liberians to manage the booths. One of the communications managers estimated that 99% were to the US, and conversations were mostly about sending money: "You hear some people shouting at the brother or sister in the States. They will say, "How can you forget your brother in Ghana suffering? Why don't you send money to help us?" Everyone wants to call their relatives in the US. They also use them to discuss the resettlement.[9]

Other services include young men hiring themselves as touts to businessmen in the market and ventures that provide various forms of transportation (bicycle rental businesses, bicycle taxi drivers, donkey cart drivers, sledges pulled by oxen). Computing and typing schools run by refugees offer courses for refugees wanting to make themselves more marketable. Water is often a problem, and in some camps, refugees have taken advantage of the demand to start water enterprises. In Budumbara camp, near Accra, refugees built reservoirs in the camp and paid for daily truckloads of water, which were then sold by the bucketful to the refugees. Or, purified water was poured into little bags in Accra, and then brought to the camp where it was purchased by water distributors and resold to other Liberian refugees as "mineral water". Those with refrigerators do particularly good business, and "little insulated coolers are strategically located all around the camp" for people to make water purchases.[10]

Sources of Cash and Credit

The sale of food and non-food rations is a popular and widespread activity, but it rarely yields enough cash to get a sustainable business going. In order to start a sustainable business that goes beyond subsistence trade, it is necessary to have access to some form of cash and credit. In camps there are few sources of credit, aside from loan programs through aid agencies, which are discussed in Chapter Three. There are no banks or microfinance institutions. Moneylenders (who are either refugees themselves or from the host community) are used occasionally, but mostly for emergencies because their interest rates are usually high. Merchants will sometimes extend credit, but usually for consumption needs only. Remittances are a highly valued source of cash, but relatively few refugees have relatives or friends in other countries that send them money. Those that do are by far the most welloff in most camps, and are often the ones with thriving businesses. For some, remittances are a regular source of support, for others, occasional transfers provide assistance but cannot be relied on to support a business. In general, remittances play a key role in maintaining the camp economy by increasing the level of cash and therefore consumption, and as a source of financing to start or sustain small business; but the flow can be intermittent and is heavily dependent on transfer companies staying in business.[11]

Most refugees must rely on their own communities to find sources of credit. One community strategy that is imported from home countries is rotating savings and credit associations, (ROSCAs). These work through a system of trust and reciprocity, and are based on small self-selected groups in which each member pays in an agreed amount each week, and then takes turns to receive the whole "pot"— which must be repaid within a designated period. These informal credit associations are well established in most parts of Africa: in West Africa they are called *susu*, in Sudan they are *sandug*, in the eastern Congo, *tontines*, in Kinshasa, they are *likilimba* or *ristournes*, and so on. However these groups are not available to everyone, as generally one must already have a source of income, such as a small business or a job in order to join. For those who are unable to find such a group, alternate sources of credit must be found, and sometimes this necessitates leaving the camp to search for sources in nearby towns.

Employment

Refugees with professional skills and higher education are more likely to move to urban areas and bypass camps altogether. But when camps are close to towns where they can work, they may prefer to live in the camp because it is cheaper and rations are available. Transportation costs to and from the town are often a problem, however. For refugees with western language skills (mainly English or French), employment with humanitarian agencies (primarily UNHCR and NGOs) is possible. Jobs with aid agencies offer both income, however small, and access to other material and nonmaterial resources, including resettlement. For refugees without skills, employment is often hard to come by outside the camp, because the local economies of host areas are often weak and unemployment high. Refugees are not the first to be hired, although since they usually accept lower wages and are more exploitable, they sometimes find "piecework," or day contracts, outside.

Con Games, Scams, Crime, and Prostitution

As in all societies, people engage in a range of illicit activities in camps. Prostitution in various forms is a livelihood strategy, but whether it is more widespread in camps than outside is not well documented. There are widespread anecdotal reports of prostitution, and some refugees see this as a more lucrative activity than petty trading—or a supplement to it.

Camp populations are easy targets for con games. In Budumburam camp, Ghana, Shelly Dick relates the case of the "Blank Money" scam:

> CMBs, or "cash money boys" are highly professional, taking a briefcase of blank bills to clients and demonstrating that the bills can be cleaned with mercury so writing for a $100 bill reappears on the blank paper. The demonstration bill is a legitimate $100 bill, but the briefcase is full of blank paper. The person watching the demonstration is asked to contribute a large sum to purchase the mercury so that the rest of the bills can be cleaned and divided between the CMBs and the client. Upon receiving money for the mercury, the CMBs then disappear.[12]

The widespread desire for resettlement is also sometimes turned into an opportunity for profit and sometimes a scam, by either actually selling places in the waiting list, or pretending to.[13]

The picture that emerges of refugees' economic activities in camps is one of diversity, in which many people participate in all kinds of ways. Like all communities, not everyone is able to engage in the economy, some are sick or traumatized or too old, and some make efforts to help these people, either through charity or by partnering with them to pool humanitarian resources. For example, in Nangweshi camp for Angolan refugees in Zambia, elderly refugees (so-called "vulnerables") were given a share of the community garden in exchange for their allotted time at the water faucet.

Constraints on the Economic Activities of Refugees in Camps

The ability of refugees in camps to engage in viable economic activities that go beyond subsistence is determined by their access to productive assets such as arable land, economic infrastructure such as mills and storage facilities, and perhaps most importantly, credit. Several factors constrain this access. One is the *physical environment and location* of the camp, including its relative isolation versus its proximity to towns and markets, and the existence of transportation infrastructure. Camps that are near towns mean better opportunities for employment and business, especially if there is public transport. But many refugee camps are in isolated, rural areas, often in insecure border zones where there is little transportation of any kind. A second constraint is *access to arable land*. Refugees with rural or agricultural backgrounds could become self-sufficient if they had access to arable land, but in most host countries, there is insufficient arable land near the camps, and what there is the local community controls. Refugees' use of land must be negotiated, either by UNHCR or the host government. Camps are deliberately sited on poor quality land, unsuited for agriculture, in order to avoid discontent on the part of the local community who could resent refugees having access to it.[14] In Kenya, both the Kakuma and Dadaab camps are in infertile, arid areas. Gaim Kibreab points out similar tendencies for settlements in eastern Sudan, noting that the age of the camp is negatively correlated with agricultural yields.[15]

Perhaps the most significant factor constraining camp refugees' access to productive assets, however, is their *freedom of movement* in and out of the camps in order to pursue economic activities. This freedom is determined by a combination of national policy and local conditions. When the host government's policy requires that refugees stay in or close to camps, they will have reduced access to work and trade opportunities. However, what actually happens at the camp level is more likely to be determined by local factors than by national level policy. Restrictive policies are difficult to implement unless they are enforced by local authorities. In Kenya, for example, refugees are officially required to stay in the camps in Kakuma and Dadaab, but large numbers move back and forth between the capital, local towns, and the camps, to trade and seek education or employment. In an increasing number of countries, restrictive policies are enforced with periodic roundups and relocations. In Tanzania, for many years a policy requiring Burundian and Congolese refugees to stay in the camps was not widely implemented, and refugees mixed with the local population. Since 2002, however, the government has tightened the law confining refugees within the camp boundaries, in a bid to cut down on crime and security problems in western Tanzania, which were largely blamed on refugees. Similar policy shifts towards increased restrictions have occurred in recent years in Pakistan, Thailand, Guinea, and elsewhere. If refugees ignore government restrictions and participate in economic activities outside camps, they become the equivalent of illegal immigrants and are often subject to harsh sanctions, including arrest and deportation.

The extent to which restrictive policies or regulations are enforced or abided by, depends on the political support—both of the government and the local community—enjoyed by the refugees. Where the host government has a stake in the conflict in the refugees' home country, and sees the refugees as supportive of the right side in that conflict, it is more likely to allow the refugees their freedom. In Pakistan, for example, the government gave Afghan refugees much greater freedoms and support in the 1980s when they were fighting the Soviet occupation (which the Pakistan government opposed), than when the Taliban came to power in the 1990s (which the Pakistan government supported).[16] If refugee numbers are relatively small, local and national authorities are more likely to turn a blind eye to their movement in and out of the camp. But if their numbers rise, or the security situation deteriorates, restrictions are more likely. Most security problems arise when conflict spills over the border, and rebels target the refugee camps but also endanger the local population. It is not an exaggeration to say that *all* host countries bordering conflict zones have experienced such incursions over the past two decades. When this happens local authorities are quick to clamp down on refugees. For example, the government of Guinea initially allowed refugees from Liberia and Sierra Leone extensive freedom of movement among the Guinean population along its borders, but when cross-border raids happened in 2000, the government required the refugees to move further from the border and to stay in camps. This pattern of initial freedom to integrate in the host community (at least in the border region) followed by increasing restrictions and relocation to camps, is widespread.

Refugees in protracted situations must also cope with shifts in attitude from the host community, which can affect both the willingness of authorities to implement restrictions, and refugees' economic activities. Over time, the local community's initial tolerance and welcoming attitude decreases, and the sense grows that the "guests are outstaying their welcome" and taking advantage of their hosts' generosity—even if the conflict continues in their home country. This shift is sometimes linked to a new influx or failed repatriation, but in general the longer a refugee population stays, the less welcoming the host community becomes. There are exceptions to this rule; some longstanding host regions like western Zambia continue to extend their welcome to Angolan refugees. However, when this shift does occur, there are economic implications for the refugees. They may have difficulty selling their goods in local town markets, or encounter more harassment form the local community and the authorities.[17] The shift in attitude is often reinforced by resentment about what is perceived as the refugees' unfair access to humanitarian assistance. As host communities become hostile and resentful, refugees are blamed for crime, loose morals, and other problems in the community. Locals may create economic obstacles, ranging from refusal to purchase goods from them to reporting them to authorities so they can be arrested or harassed.[18]

In countries where restrictive policies are absent or not enforced, refugees can work outside camps, but only after obtaining permits to leave the camp. Permission to leave the camp or settlement is usually obtained relatively easily from the government official in charge, but work permits must be obtained in the capital. This means refugees must first get a permit to leave the camp, then travel to the capital, get the work permit, find a job, and travel back to the camp before the travel permit expires. In Mozambique, in order for asylum-seekers to retain legal status in the country, they must renew their documents every two months. These kinds of documentation requirements are prohibitively expensive, both in time and money. In addition, the distance from camps of many registration sites make them effectively inaccessible, so that legal work outside the camps is not an option for many refugees.[19]

Factors Enabling the Economic Activities of Refugees in Camps: Humanitarian Inputs

Although refugees in camps face restrictions on their movements, they receive free goods in the form of humanitarian assistance, and thus are at an economic advantage compared with both the local people and self-settled refugees living outside camps. Humanitarian assistance takes the form of both food aid and non-food aid, such as seeds and tools, health services, shelter, water and sanitation, and education. Many relief agencies implement programs aimed at supporting refugees livelihoods, either to encourage self-reliance as humanitarian assistance decreases, or to support repatriation. These programs include agriculture, vocational training, income generating programs such as microcredit, or in-kind loans (such as seeds and tools) to support agriculture, livestock, and small businesses. We will discuss these kinds of programs in Chapter Three.

Humanitarian input also comes in the form of economic infrastructure, such as transportation and transit facilities, the creation and maintenance of road and communication networks, electricity generators and so forth, which supports and expands the camp economy. The arrival of international relief agencies is accompanied by communication infrastructure like satellite dishes, radio networks, and computers, some of which can be utilized by refugees. One of the most significant economic inputs provided by relief agencies is transportation. The trucks and four-wheel drive vehicles used by relief agencies constitute one of the most valued commodities in developing countries; and refugees, who rarely have access to efficient transport, find ways to gain access to them. Trucks are sometimes hired by groups of refugees, usually as part of income generating programs, to collect wood, or to transport traders and goods to town markets. UNHCR organizes repatriation convoys or "go and see" expeditions, in which a group of refugees is invited to visit the home country to assess current conditions there and report back to their compatriots when they return; these journeys may also be made for marketing or trading purposes.

The presence of international agencies may also serve as a form of security, which, in turn, can increase the economic viability of camps. Even if UNHCR and NGOs cannot physically protect refugees, their presence can act as a deterrent to abuses and crime. Although reported incidents of fraud, abuse, and harassment over the years have caused some serious breakdowns of trust in both UNHCR and NGOs, camps still represent an international presence in otherwise remote regions; and although camps are not always safe, they are often safer than living on the outside.

The availability of humanitarian aid and related inputs is a significant factor in the economy of refugee camps—and it affects the cost-benefit calculation of economically active refugees' decision as to whether to live in the camps or not.[20] In economists' terms, refugees are receiving a free or public good, which partly explains why many refugees base themselves and their families in the camp, even if it means a difficult and expensive commute to work. In general, refugees with professional skills and higher education are more likely to move to urban areas than to stay in camps, but when camps are near towns, they may prefer to live in the camp, especially if they have families, who can then have access to assistance.

Humanitarian inputs increase the economic viability of camps, but it is important to recognize that access to these inputs is highly contested, and once control over their distribution is acquired, it is jealously guarded. For example, deciding who should control food aid distribution in camps is very controversial, because of the power it bestows on the distributors. Should the refugees themselves control food distribution? But if so, who among them? Refugee camps are not democratic institutions, and in some camps, self-proclaimed "leaders" emerge and take control of food distribution, but do not represent the best interests of all the refugees. On the other hand, where refugee leaders are recognized and accepted by the refugees, they can impose a fair distributive system in the camps, or at least one that is acceptable to most refugees. Some argue that a highly exploitable resource like food distribution should not be managed by refugees but by neutral aid agencies. The problem here is that aid agencies often hire refugees to work in camps; indeed, agency employment is one of the most desirable and highly contested resources. Humanitarian aid is also used to try to control the location of refugees and to enforce encampment policy. Host governments often require that only refugees in camps be eligible for humanitarian assistance, and these goods are not available to those outside the camps, or only in smaller amounts.[21] For example, until 2003, the government of Mozambique allowed urban refugees in Maputo to receive humanitarian assistance, but after it relocated all refugees to the camp near Nampula (about 800 miles north of Maputo), assistance was only available in the camp and urban refugees were denied access to humanitarian programs.[22]

Camps as Hubs of Economic Activity: The Economic Impact on the Host Area

The economies of camps are not limited to the confines of the camp. Refugees move out into the surrounding community to pursue trade and seek employment, and locals enter the camp in search of cheap labor, business opportunities, and investment. Many refugees live in the camps where their families reside, and work outside, commuting back and forth. Locals living outside the camp are sometimes employed by aid agencies—or even by refugees. Local farmers or development projects look-ing for cheap labor may also hire refugees. Outside the camps, refugees' economic success depends on demand in the local economy, the willingness of local authori-ties to look the other way when government policy forbids refugee employment, and the willingness of the local population to engage with them economically.

The economic and security infrastructure rendered through humanitarian aid is intended to serve camps and the logistical needs of the relief industry. However, infrastructures such as roads and communication services intended to serve the humanitarian agencies also serve the local community, and can help to reduce the isolation of camps and increase the economic potential of the host area. A good road can make a great difference—by rendering an area accessible it stimulates the growth of markets and trading. Many aid agencies offer services like health clinics and schools to locals, and indeed, this approach is seen as a way to reduce local resent-ment and thereby increase refugees' ability to engage in economic activities in the community. The case of Sembakounya camp in Guinea is illustrative:

> Although the neighboring communities are ambivalent about the presence
> of the refugees, they recognize the changes and development brought along
> with the construction of the camp. Refugees provide a cheap and welcome
> source of wage labor on people's farms. The need to transport large, heavy
> loads of humanitarian relief supplies to the camp has led to the recon-
> struction of the road, which provides locals with bountiful job opportuni-
> ties where there had been none before...The increase of 7,600 refugees in
> the consumer population has encouraged traders to bring all kinds of
> goods, both local and exotic.[23]

When host governments make economic arguments promoting encampment policies, they base them on the belief that refugees compete with locals for jobs. There is now growing evidence that the positive economic contribution made by refugees in the form of economic stimulus, as well as humanitarian assistance, can outweigh the problem of increased competition. Of course, employers are in favor of this kind of competition, even if local workers are not, and it is employers rather than workers who tend to have more political influence with governments. When refugees are forced to stay in camps they are less able to pursue livelihoods, more vul-nerable to unreliable arrivals of humanitarian assistance, less able to exercise their rights, and more susceptible to control by political forces. These difficulties do not benefit host communities and increase the risk of security or crime problems. If refugees must live in camps, they should be permitted to move in and out freely, in order to pursue livelihoods. We will return to this discussion in Chapter Six. In many host countries, a significant proportion of refugees stay away from official settlement sites and camps, and self-settle in rural areas, especially near the borders, where they live without registering with the authorities, and thus without status. An increasing number move to urban areas. As we discuss in the next chapter, the problems they encounter there tend to be much greater than those encountered in border areas, but for many urban refugees these difficulties are still preferable to staying in camps.

Notes

1   There is a large library on this topic, see for example, Anderson, *Do No Harm*; Fiona Terry, *Condemned to Repeat?: The Paradox of Humanitarian Action* (Ithaca and London: Cornell University Press, 2002); Stephen John Stedman and Fred Tanner, eds., *Refugee Manipulation: War, Politics, and the Abuse of Human Suffering* (Washington, DC: Brookings Institution Press, 2003).

2   Crisp, "No Solutions."

3   USCR, *Pakistan*.

4   For discussions of refugee trading activities in and around camps, see Marc-Antoine Pérouse de Montclos and Peter Mwangi Kagwanja, "Refugee Camps or Cities? Camps in Northern Kenya," *Journal of Refugee Studies* Vol 13. No. 2 (2000): 205-222; Agnes Callamard, "Refugees and Local Hosts: A Study of the Trading Interactions Between Mozambican Refugees and Malawian Villagers," *Journal of Refugee Studies* 7(1) (1994): 23.

5   The food aid industry is controlled by the World Food Programme (WFP) the biggest humanitarian agency in the world, which manages procurement, distribution, and all related programs. In 2003, WFP's various divisions purchased US$634 million of food aid and US$179 million worth of goods and services. Not all of this went to refugees. See www.wfp.org/index.asp ?section=5.

6   B. Lacey Andrews, *When Is a Refugee Not a Refugee? Refugee/Host Relations in Guinea*, report no. 88, United Nations High Commissioner for Refugees (UNHCR) Evaluation and Policy Analysis Unit (EPAU) series, 2003; available at www.unhcr.ch.

7   According to Lacey Andrews (9), in Sembakounya camp (Guinea), a WFP spokesperson warned that there was to be no selling of the food distribution right outside the supply center. The head of WFP had seen two trucks leaving after the last supply day filled with USAID-marked sacks of food and tins of oil. There were also to be new guidelines for how the food would be distributed: A refugee could not pick up food for someone else, not even the handicapped, only one ration card per person would be filled, and the cards of people who left had to be returned to avoid stolen coupons or sold coupons.

8   Andrews, "When Is a Refugee Not a Refugee?" 9-10.

9   Shelly Dick, "Liberians in Ghana: Living without Humanitarian Assistance," (working paper, New Issues in Refugee Research, no. 57, UNHCR, 2002), 28-29.

10   Dick, "Liberians in Ghana," 28-29.

11   Dick, "Liberians in Ghana," 30. For more on the consequences of remittances for refugees and conflict-affected countries, see Ismail Ahmed,

"Remittances and Their Economic Impact in Post-war Somaliland," *Disasters* 24 (2000): 380-389; Khalid Koser and Nicholas Van Hear, "Asylum Migration: Implications for Countries of Origin," *United Nations University/World Institute for Development Economics Research Discussion Paper* DP 2003/20, February 2003; Cindy Horst and Nicholas Van Hear, "Counting the Cost: Refugees, Remittances and the 'War Against Terrorism'," *Forced Migration Review*, No. 14, (2002): 32-34.

12   Dick, "Liberians in Ghana," 33fn.

13   For refugees seeking resettlement in the United States, "selling places" on the affidavit of relationship (AOR) for P3 family reunification resettlement is common. The process for P3 resettlement begins when an anchor, a refugee in the United States, fills out an AOR listing all the eligible family members he or she wishes to bring to the United States. These individuals listed on the affidavit are interviewed in the camp by the resettlement agency (the JVA). If one of these persons is not in the camp at the time of the scheduled interview, other family members sometimes sell that space to the highest bidder. According to UNHCR Ghana, a place on the AOR can be sold for as high as $2,000. Dick, "Liberians in Ghana," 30.

14   According to Pérouse de Montclos and Kagwanja (207), in the case of Kenya: "The government feared that the refugees might become settled in valuable areas of the country, especially in the highlands. Accordingly, the Kakuma and Dadaab camps were located in a semi-arid environment with a [population] density of less than 0.05 inhabitants per hectare, compared with 5 in rural districts like Kisii."

15   Gaim Kibreab, "Refugees in the Sudan: Unresolved Issues," in *African Refugees: Development Aid and Repatriation,* ed. Howard Adelman and John Sorenson (Boulder, CO: Westview Press, 1994), 49-52.

16   USCR, *Pakistan.*

17   For example, in Ghana, "Liberian women refugees claimed that when they tried to sell things in Ghanaian markets, the Ghanaians stopped to buy something but when they heard the distinctive accent of Liberian English...they walked away without making a purchase. In response, the Liberian women established a market center at the entrance of the camp." Dick, "Liberians in Ghana," 30.

18   Dick, "Liberians in Ghana," 33.

19   For more on the host government policies of Kenya see Hyndman and Viktor-Nylund, "UNHCR and the Status of *Prima Facie* Refugees in Kenya," *International Journal of Refugee Law* 10(1/2):21-48; and Pérouse de Montclos and Kagwanja, "Refugee Camps or Cities?" For Tanzania see Loren Landau, "Beyond the Losers: Transforming Governmental Practice in Refugee-Affected Tanzania," *Journal of Refugee Studies* Vol. 16(1) (2003):19-43; Roos Willems "The Refugee Experience: Forced Migration and Social

Networks in Dar Es Salaam, Tanzania," Ph.D. Dissertation, (Anthropology), Graduate School, University of Florida (2003). For Uganda, see Dryden-Peterson and Hovil, "Local Integration."

20   Eric Werker, "Refugees in Kyangwali Settlement: Constraints on Economic Freedom," (working paper, Refugee Law Project, no. 7, 2002).

21   As Kibreab (48) notes of the Sudan, "Although the number of refugees in the organized settlements is small, most international aid is directed to them, to the neglect of the self-settled refugees."

22   Anna Mecagni, *World Relief's Income Generation Animal Husbandry Program, Maratane Refugee Camp, Mozambique*, Alchemy Project Country Report No. 5, August 2004; available at www.famine.tufts.edu.

23   Andrews, "When Is a Refugee Not a Refugee?" 9-10.

Chapter 3
Urban Refugees

We tend to think of refugees in developing countries as living in camps or settlements, but a growing number move to the cities and towns of host countries.[1] According to official figures of UNHCR, 18 percent of all persons of concern to UNHCR worldwide lived in urban areas in 2002, up from thirteen percent in 2001 and just one percent five years earlier.[2] The official number of such people in 2002 is over 2.4 million, but this does not include the vastly greater number of refugees who have not declared themselves to UNHCR or the host government. Compared with their co-nationals in camps, urban refugees often face greater protection risks, and receive less support in terms of shelter, health care, education, and other social services—and sometimes none at all. Still, many refugees prefer to live in urban areas than in camps. How do they survive? As with the preceding chapter on camps, we will focus on the refugees themselves, their strategies for economic survival, and the consequences for urban areas.

As the number of urban refugees grows, both absolutely and as a proportion of the people of concern to UNHCR, researchers are paying more attention to them, and to the problems and opportunities they present to host governments and communities. There is now growing literature on the subject, both in the forced migration field and in urban studies, demography and anthropology, and several research projects on urban refugees in the south.[3] This chapter draws extensively on a study of forced migrants in Johannesburg, in which the author and Loren Landau have been engaged since 2002. In February 2003 we conducted a survey in Johannesburg exploring the experiences of both forced migrants and South Africans.[4] In many ways, Johannesburg is representative of the urban experience of African refugees. South Africa hosts more than 105,000 refugees, of whom some 26,000 are legally recognized refugees and more than 78,000 are asylum-seekers. They are from all over Africa, and mostly live in urban areas, as South Africa does not have refugee camps. Despite South Africa's relative wealth and development, urban refugees encounter many of the same problems in Johannesburg as in other African cities and cities of the global South. As we did in the survey, this chapter explores whether being a refugee carries with it particular difficulties not faced by the urban poor among whom refugees and other migrants usually live. Here we also explore whether it makes sense to consider urban refugees separately from other kinds of migrants.

Definition, Patterns of Distribution, and Demographics

Urban refugees are self-settled refugees—formally recognized or not—residing in urban areas. In the sprawling and destitute migrant communities of many of the world's capitals, it is difficult to separate the refugees—those who flee persecution—from those who migrate for economic or other reasons. The livelihood problems facing all urban poor, whether displaced or not, are similar; the difference for urban refugees and migrants is that they face additional problems related to their legal status and to xenophobia that affect their ability to pursue livelihoods.

Refugees often flee to towns and cities that are in or near conflict zones, like Kabul, Afghanistan; Peshawar, Pakistan; Khartoum, Sudan; Kampala, Uganda; Bujumbura, Burundi; Goma, Congo-Kinshasa (Democratic Republic of Congo); and Luanda, Angola. But even cities that are relatively distant from conflict have experienced significant influxes in recent years, including Cairo, Nairobi, New Delhi, Bangkok, and Johannesburg. Many cities in or near conflict zones, such as Kabul and Luanda, also contain large numbers of their own citizens who have been forcibly displaced by conflict, or who are returnees from displacement. In some host countries, different refugee nationalities live in different locations. For example, in India, Sri Lankan and Tibetan refugees are required to live in camps, but Afghan refugees are in urban areas—mainly New Delhi, where, although the Indian government regards them as economic migrants, they receive assistance from UNHCR.

Urban refugees find their way to towns and cities for various reasons. It is widely assumed that most are from urban socio-economic backgrounds and choose to come to towns because they cannot farm or pursue livelihoods in rural areas and camps. Refugees also leave camps because they become frustrated in their goal of resettlement. In her study of refugees in Dar es Salaam, Roos Willems explains how the desire for resettlement made refugees leave the camps in western Tanzania and head for the city:

> many of the refugees are unaware of the very strict selection criteria and procedures of both UNHCR and the resettlement countries and consider it "their right" as refugees to be resettled. Feeling cut off from the rest of the world for lack of modern means of communication and tired of waiting, a considerable number of refugees leave the camps and head for Dar es Salaam, expecting in vain, that it will be easier to "push their case through" by knocking on the doors of the UNHCR's Head Office.[5]

While some urban refugees spend time in camps, many come directly to the city without accessing humanitarian assistance along the way. In our Johannesburg survey, we found that just six percent of our sample had ever stayed in a refugee camp, and only two percent reported receiving aid from an international organization.[6]

In Africa, studies in Kampala, Dar es Salaam and Johannesburg have found that urban refugees tend to be younger males of urban background.[7] Those forced migrants in our sample who made it to Johannesburg were considerably younger than the host population, with only five percent above the age of forty compared to twenty-two percent of South Africans. They were also predominantly male (seventy-one percent vs. forty-seven percent for South Africans) and far fewer had children: sixty-four percent of migrants reported having no children as opposed to thirty-five percent of the South Africans. Just under eighty percent of all the forced migrants surveyed reported living in cities for most of their lives before coming to South Africa, and another seventeen percent had spent the greater part of their lives in towns. Less than four percent claimed rural origins.

In other cities, refugee demographic profiles vary. In New Delhi, one study found that slightly more than half of the Afghan refugees were female and that, unlike the first asylum-seekers who came to India after the Soviet invasion of Afghanistan in 1979, the refugees there in 2000 were not educated professionals or prosperous urban traders. According to UNHCR:

> A considerable proportion of those who remain in New Delhi are more recent arrivals, traders and shopkeepers of rural origin who fled to Kabul and other urban areas to escape the fighting, and who subsequently moved on to the Indian capital. Around 60 per cent are illiterate.[8]

Refugees also move to urban centers when food aid is cut off in camps. In Pakistan, in the mid-1990s, one unintended consequence of UNHCR's and the World Food Programme's decision to cut off food aid to camp residents—a consequence that the Pakistani government neither anticipated nor welcomed—was that tens (perhaps hundreds) of thousands of refugees subsequently migrated to the cities in search of work.[9]

The Institutional Context: Host Government Policy and Humanitarian Assistance

In countries of first asylum in the South, most governments adopt the position that those in camps are *prima facie* refugees, and those who come to urban areas are economic migrants. In many situations, even UNHCR assumes that those who make it to cities can support themselves—otherwise they would have stayed in camps where assistance was available.[10] This belief that so-called "irregular movers" have moved voluntarily means authorities generally do not offer them permanent asylum or resettlement, or much in the way of humanitarian assistance in urban areas.[11] According to UNHCR, irregular movers are:

> refugees, whether they have been formally identified as such or not (asylum-seekers), who move in an irregular manner from countries in which *they have already found protection,* in order to seek asylum or permanent resettlement elsewhere.[12]

UNHCR policy then clarifies,

> if a refugee or asylum seeker has moved from a country of first asylum *without legitimate reasons,* the person *should not normally be considered for assistance,* with the obvious exception of life-saving assistance that is not available in a timely manner from another source.[13]

Nevertheless, according to the UNHCR Policy on Urban Refugees, the agency "should promote the refugees' right to work and access to national services, wherever possible." The 1951 Convention requires states to consider the claims of asylum-seekers regardless of the route they took. The issue of irregular movers is particularly relevant to South Africa, where Zimbabwe is the only bordering country sending refugees. Most refugees have passed through other countries to reach South Africa.

Host governments are rarely able to prevent the arrival of urban refugees, but they can deny them permission to work and any form of assistance. In Cairo, the government does not permit refugees to work, and residence is granted on the understanding that needy cases will be assisted by UNHCR for the duration of their stay.[14] In Tanzania and Kenya, authorities require refugees to live in camps or settlements and view urban refugees as illegal migrants. Those who leave the camps do so at their own risk. The authorities tolerate them sometimes, but they are always in legal jeopardy. Other countries (usually those with smaller numbers of refugees) adopt a more benign approach. In Mozambique, refugees are permitted to remain in a camp where relief agencies meet their basic needs until they can support themselves; they are then allowed to move to the cities (with formal permission). In host countries where camps are near urban areas, like Mozambique and Ghana, refugees often commute between the camp and the town in order to trade or work. They use the camp as a base, or a place where other family members can remain while they pursue livelihoods. In Uganda, the government allows a small number of registered refugees to live and work in Kampala as long as they do not request assistance. This group is made up of professionals, skilled individuals, and people supported by relatives. In addition, an unknown number of refugees have self-settled in Kampala without registering with the authorities.[15]

In countries where registered refugees are permitted to live in urban areas, such as South Africa and Egypt, there is relatively little official humanitarian assistance available compared to what is provided in the camps.[16] In general, neither host governments nor UNHCR want refugees in urban areas, because providing assistance and protection is more expensive and politically difficult than keeping them in camps. Aid organizations are concerned that local resentment and increased xenophobia will occur if self-settled refugees are entitled to assistance, but the impoverished community among which the refugees live is not. In Johannesburg, relatively few refugees are eligible for humanitarian assistance, and most struggle to meet their basic needs, including shelter and food. Although there are a few mutual aid refugee associations and local nongovernmental organizations that seek to assist and advise refugees, they lack support. In some countries, including India and Egypt, UNHCR has provided a monthly subsistence allowance to the most needy.[17] But allowances for refugees can create resentment on the part of host populations who are equally poor and affected by conflict, but not eligible for humanitarian support.

Most urban refugees do not seek out humanitarian assistance, and do not register with UNHCR. In Pakistan, in 1996, only 16,000 of the 40,000 new arrivals sought UNHCR help. In 2000, more than 172,000 Afghans entered Pakistan flee-ing heavy fighting in the north and the widening effects of a severe drought. Many refugees stayed with relatives or moved to cities throughout Pakistan without regis-tering with the authorities or seeking assistance.[18] This pattern is widespread, and as urban migration grows we are likely to see increased numbers of refugees in the cities of the south.

Pursuing Urban Livelihoods

With little or no help from the state or humanitarian agencies, urban refugees engage in different livelihood strategies. Recent studies show how urban refugees and migrants survive and even prosper, compared with their co-nationals who remain in camps.[19] Social networks of co-nationals help refugees find employment, housing, and sources of credit. Friends and relatives in the diaspora in other countries send cash. But the economic activities of urban refugees do not reflect their education lev-els and business or professional experience. Instead, they are obliged to engage in a range of informal sector activities, broadly divided between self-employment in trade and services, and some form of paid employment. Few refugees work full-time in either the formal or informal sector. In the Johannesburg sample, one third (thirty-two percent) of South Africans reported working full time in either the formal or informal sector, compared with only seven percent of the migrants. Of those in our sample who were working, over a quarter (twenty-eight percent) of the migrants claimed to be self-employed, compared with six percent of South Africans. When asked what kind of work they would like to be doing, given their training and work experience, twenty-four percent of our non-South African respondents described professional work ("doctor," "lawyer," "journalist/media professional," or "other pro-fessional"), and twenty-six percent described themselves as businesspersons.

Informal Sector Activities: Microenterprise

For economically active urban refugees, informal small businesses of various kinds offer some income. These include trade in small goods and services, and range in size from hawking a few wares on the street to small stores. Many refugees start their own business as carpenters, shoemakers, hairdressers, telephone kiosk operators, craft makers, and tailors. Sometimes these are new occupations for them, and they rely on friends and networks to provide training or funds for training. In the Johan-nesburg survey, petty trading (hawking) was forced migrants' most significant occu-pation (twenty-one percent against less than one percent for South Africans). The income from such activities tends to be limited and unpredictable, and street traders who work outside risk theft, violent robbery, and police harassment.

Despite these problems, a small number of refugee entrepreneurs flourish, and they are often a source of economic rejuvenation in areas that otherwise lack resources and have been largely abandoned by the formal sector. In Johannesburg, most formal businesses have fled the inner city, but a variety of thriving businesses have sprung up, owned and run by refugees. A panel beating shop (in the United States, known as a body shop) owned and run by Burundian refugees services ten cars a week. A small shoe-making factory makes quality shoes, and also provides vocational training for a small number of refugees and South Africans. With a loan from a NGO, a Kenyan refugee woman has started a bead business, making jewelry and Christmas decorations, that employs three other people. Many refugee entrepreneurs become employers, providing work to nationals and other refugees. Our survey found that, of those who are economically active, a significant number of refugees had employed other people. When asked, "Since coming to South Africa, have you ever paid someone to do work for you?" thirty-four percent of the non-South Africans said yes, compared with twenty-one percent of South Africans. Of the Ethiopians, almost sixty percent had employed people—most of them South Africans rather than other migrants.

Obstacles to the Economic Activities of Urban Refugees

Urban refugees face the same economic problems as the urban poor: shortages of jobs, housing, credit and banking services, higher prevalence of crime, and political marginalization. Refugees and asylum-seekers face additional challenges. Having borrowed money to make their journeys or because they are living on the goodwill of locals, they often owe large debts to family members or others. The authorities restrict refugees' right to work, grant little or no public assistance, and require documentation. In addition, the local population and law enforcement agencies often react to refugees, as to urban migrants generally, with xenophobia—ranging from ignorance and resentment to harassment and violence. The next section focuses on four of the main economic obstacles facing urban refugees: housing, documentation, xenophobia and access to financial services.

Housing

In rapidly growing cities, finding decent and affordable housing is a serious problem for all urban poor, and migrants often have to pay more for accommodation. Government slum clearance programs limit self-built housing in shantytowns or peri-urban settlements—that is, areas on the outskirts of cities—reducing the supply of low-cost housing. In many cases, people are not given advance warning about slum clearance, nor are they compensated when their residences are condemned. Policy makers often consider informal settlements illegal, and are unlikely to adequately compensate or assist their residents with alternatives. Refugees must compete in the low-cost housing market without enough money for a deposit, local references, or permanent employment. Local or national housing regulations that require proof of residence or citizenship make housing more expensive for them than for other urban poor. Sharing accommodation with unknown families—a common survival strategy—can pose the risk of disease, theft, and physical or sexual violence. Urban refugee families often must sublet rooms with another household, or they must find a landlord willing to grant a short-term contract at a premium price. Those not able to find any housing end up on city streets exposed to even greater risk.

Refugees' housing strategies include frequent relocation, and the associated time, expense, and psychological uncertainty can affect their livelihood strategies. Frequent relocation retards the ability to build social capital—the personal networks necessary to find employment and gain access to schools and other social services.

Identification and Documentation

Even in countries like South Africa and Egypt, which allow refugees to be in urban areas, obtaining and renewing refugee identity documents and work and travel permits are a constant burden, which requires long hours and expense. If the government does not renew their documents regularly, refugees can be jailed or forced to pay bribes in order to prevent arrest. Police frequently shake down refugee entrepreneurs for bribes in urban areas. Without papers, refugees are unable to sign leases, open bank accounts, cash checks, or seek formal employment.

Where refugees are entitled to services, they may be unaware of their rights, and there are few organizations to inform them. Refugees often cannot get legitimate travel documents from their home countries, lose them in flight, or must leave them behind. Without them refugees cannot easily cross borders—a serious obstacle in countries where much of the trade is international. In some countries, even Convention Travel Documents are not widely recognized by service providers or the authorities.

In host countries where refugees are allowed to work, they need to get work permits or business licenses, which in turn need to be renewed. This process requires fees, travel fare, and time off from work. Although refugees often work for lower wages, employers are wary of hiring them if they don't recognize their papers or are unsure about their right to work. Employers may also question refugees' long-term commitment or qualifications, and refugees often lack references. Article 19 of the Refugee Convention allows for the practice of professions, but refugees who are doctors, lawyers, accountants, and other professionals often lack local credentials. Many skilled or professional refugees in urban areas are unable to work in the formal sector because they lack certification in the host country, or because employers do not recognize their foreign qualifications. Credentials from their native country are usually not valid without additional training or local certification. Other barriers to refugee employment—even when their papers are in order—include inability to speak the local language, straightforward discrimination, or an employer's belief that the presence of a foreigner will turn away customers.

Xenophobia, Competition with Locals and Encounters with Authorities

Xenophobia, or anti-foreigner hostility by the local population, is a common experience for urban refugees, although the degree of intensity and the forms it takes vary from one country to another. Locals see refugees as responsible for crime, as vectors of disease, as competitors for jobs and customers, and as a threat to cultural values. The situation in Pakistan is typical of many host countries:

> In Pakistan, local people, the local media, and Pakistani government officials blame Afghan refugees living in the cities (both those who migrated from the camps and those who never lived in camps) for many of the social and economic woes plaguing Pakistan's cities. Muhammad Haroon Shaukat, a director general in the Ministry of Foreign Affairs, told USCR, "The refugees have caused social problems, including an increase in crime, drug addiction and drug trafficking, and illegal trade. Local people say that the Afghans take their jobs and drive up real estate prices." Another official said, "Kalashnikovs and automatic weapons were introduced into Pakistan because of the refugees. Drugs were introduced because of them. And, I am extremely sorry to say this, but a great deal of prostitution began. Refugees work for less, so they create unemployment for local people. I grew up in Peshawar. Conditions in the city are much worse than before."[20]

In addition to the potential for violence, xenophobic attitudes and harassment hurt refugees' income and stability as a result of petty harassment, extortion, and discrimination in hiring, housing, and access to services like health and education. When local vendors are unhappy about competition with refugees they complain to local authorities, who then remove the refugee businesses.

Authorities often tolerate, and may in some cases encourage, police harassment or even vigilante justice against refugees, including violence, illegal detention, or deportation. While in most cities the police perennially raid informal businesses and try to prevent hawking and other forms of street trading, authorities are often more likely to come down harder on immigrants—seizing their goods or asking them to pay bribes or other forms of protection money—especially if they lack proper documentation. In Johannesburg, we found that migrants were far more likely to be victims of crime or police harassment than South Africans. Despite being in the country for a shorter time than natives, seventy-two percent of the migrants surveyed reported that they or someone they lived with had been a victim of crime, compared with forty-three percent of South Africans. Rather than protecting foreigners, police often contribute to the problem. When asked if they had ever been stopped by the police, seventy-one percent of migrants responded affirmatively, compared with twenty percent of South Africans. Most of the time, police stop people to check immigration and identity documents, but forced migrants report having their papers taken and even destroyed by the police. Many spoke of paying bribes to avoid arrest and possible deportation.

Local people widely believe migrants to be responsible for urban crime. In our survey, most South Africans who thought crime in the city was increasing believed that immigrants were among the primary perpetrators. But neither police statistics nor survey evidence supports this. The Director of the South African Metro Police at the Hillbrow Police Station told us that only some seven percent of those arrested for crimes were foreigners, which is below the percentage of foreigners in the area.[21] The police said that foreigners living in Johannesburg are overwhelmingly the victims, rather than the perpetrators of crime.

Access to Credit and Financial Services[22]

Many urban refugees are dependent on small business to make a living, but their start-up costs are often higher—and the start-up phase longer—than for locals. For example, in Dar es Salaam, landlords require twelve months rent paid upfront.[23] Lack of credit and other financial difficulties are serious economic constraints when trying to start or expand a small business. Urban areas have more banks and credit facilities than do camps or rural areas, but refugees do not generally have access to their services.[24] In Johannesburg, the main obstacle to opening a bank account is obtaining a Refugee Identity Document issued by the Department of Home Affairs. Possession of a Refugee ID book (which looks like the ID book all South Africans carry, but is maroon-colored) does not guarantee credit, but South African banks do not generally permit refugees to open an account without one. All refugees are entitled to free ID books under the 1998 Refugee Act, but the majority of legally recognized refugees in South Africa do not have one, because there is a large backlog. According to a study by UNHCR in South Africa in 2002, only eleven percent of refugees hold maroon identity books.[25] Asylum-seekers—whose refugee status has not yet been granted—possess only Section 22 permits, which cannot be used to open a bank account. If their cases were resolved in six months as the law provides, the denial of bank accounts might be tolerable, but the asylum process can take up to a year or more.[26]

In most host countries, refugees have almost no access to credit—they cannot open bank accounts or get loans—and have few safe places to keep their cash and assets. Traditional sources of credit, such as extended family networks or the social capital found in home communities, are absent, or soon exhausted. Some are able to get start-up loans from religious and humanitarian assistance organizations, or from relatives and friends—both in the area and abroad. In Cairo, a UNHCR study of urban refugees found that remittances from Sudanese and Somali diaspora communities in the Gulf States, Europe, North America, and Australia are an important source of revenue.[27] However, it is likely that families in the diaspora might be less willing to send money to their displaced relatives in urban areas, because they believe that they are more capable of surviving than their kin in camps or still in the home country. This is still an unexplored area of research.

Moneylenders charge high interest rates and can exert rough repayment demands, but they are easily accessible and have uncomplicated loan terms. Refugees often use moneylenders to engage in quick turnover petty trade. A refugee borrows money from a moneylender at an agreed interest rate and purchases a small amount of goods, such as vegetables, cigarettes, or candy, from the market outside of town where prices are somewhat lower. This often requires a long, early-morning journey to the market and transportation costs. The goods are then brought into the town center and sold to passersby for a slightly higher price. Once the goods have been disposed of, the trader returns to the moneylender, repays the loan with interest, and clears a small amount—usually only enough to purchase food for the family's evening meal. The process is then repeated the next day. This daily grind enables household subsistence at best, and is rarely enough to enable a refugee to clear outstanding debts or to generate enough profit to start one's own business.

Refugees are effectively forced to work in a cash economy. Without credit or safe places to keep their money, they must carry their goods and daily earnings with them, and are frequently targets of street crime and—especially given their awkward legal status—police extortion. People living in shared or insecure housing, or who work outside (e.g., hawking, construction, cleaning) are particularly vulnerable to theft and xenophobic violence.

Explaining Refugees' Entrepreneurial Success

Given the barriers faced by urban refugees, the success of many refugee entrepreneurs in urban centers demands explanation. Self-selection brings the most entrepreneurial and educated to cities, and there is some evidence that urban refugees have higher levels of education and skills than the host community. Many of the more successful urban refugee entrepreneurs had business experience in their home countries: more than twenty-eight percent of Ethiopians and twenty-six percent of Somalis in the Johannesburg study reported owning businesses in their country of origin. Much of their success can also be explained by refugees' ability and willingness to exploit niche skills in existing markets. Urban refugees often bring with them new or different skills, more business experience than their local counterparts, and knowledge of markets in their home countries. In Maputo and Johannesburg, the refugees' skills in sewing traditional African clothes and in woodcarving have proved highly marketable. Refugees' knowledge of markets in other African countries gives them an advantage in undertaking import-export activities. Many Congolese refugees in Johannesburg, for example, support their livelihoods by sending goods from South Africa to the Democratic Republic of the Congo, and receiving Congolese crafts to sell locally.

It is also possible that lack of access to public assistance and formal employment opportunities make refugees more willing to take financial risks to make their businesses work. As a result, many have expanded microenterprises into small businesses—some of which employ local people—in a relatively short period of time.

Conclusion

Urban refugees can easily be an economic asset, rather than a burden. Developing countries need to harness the economic power of the informal sector by smoothing the passage of informal sector businesses into the formal sector. Urban refugees are a good example of a potential win-win situation for both host countries and refugees.

Many urban refugees are entrepreneurs whose economic contributions to the city can be maximized by implementing their rights to work and to freedom of movement. Government authorities that create obstacles to refugees' livelihoods—through backlogs of status determination procedures or police harassment—not only prevent refugees from pulling their economic weight, they create environments of resentment and rule breaking. By speeding up access to refugee status, as well as providing simple improvements in opening doors to credit, bank accounts, and recertification procedures, governments and the corporate sector can smooth the way into the formal sector, where refugee businesses can be taxed and regulated. The situation described by an Eritrean refugee in Johannesburg benefits neither the host country nor the refugees:

> You know, for those of us in the inner city, there are really two governments. The big one [the South African government] doesn't collect any taxes from us. The other one, the one on the street, collects at least twenty grand every time we use the street.[28]

Host governments would do well to ensure that only one government operates in the refugee- and migrant- dominated inner city, and that this is one that both protects refugees' rights and benefits from their economic skills. Donor states and relief agencies ought to consider encouraging and enabling host countries to ease up on urban refugees. One way to do this would be for donors to offer to compensate host countries for reasonable expenses to their public health, education, and other social support systems that benefit refugees. This support should not take the form of parallel relief structures and special services for refugees, but should supplement existing national services. In addition, donors should consider supporting vocational education, microfinance, and other services that support urban refugee livelihoods, but which most urban refugees cannot afford or access. Even if such support was spread out over all the urban poor—but explicitly conditioned upon full enjoyment of Convention rights for refugees among them—it would still be cheaper than typical refugee care and maintenance. And even if it weren't cheaper, what does it mean for the international community to say that refugees have rights, but do nothing to ensure that they enjoy them?

Notes

1   This chapter was published as "Just Enough for the City: Urban Refugees Make Their Own Way" in *World Refugee Survey,* 2004 by the USCRI.

2   UNHCR statistics for 2002 can be found on their Web site. For the 1995 figure, see paragraph six of "UNHCR's Policy and Practice Regarding Urban Refugees, A Discussion Paper," written in 1995, and found on their EPAU Web site at www.unhcr.ch.

3   See Loren Landau's "Study Guide to Urban Refugees." *FMO Research Guide: Study Guide to Urban Refugees* (February 2004); available at www.forced migration.org/guides/fmo024/.

4   For more on the project's sampling strategy and logistical challenges see, Karen Jacobsen and Loren Landau, "The Dual Imperative in Refugee Research: Some Methodological and Ethical Considerations in Social Science Research on Forced Migration," *Disasters* Vol. 27 (3) 2003: 185-206. For a report on our findings, see Landau and Jacobsen, "Refugees in the New Johannesburg," *Forced Migration Review 19*, (January 2004): 44-46.

5   Roos Willems, "The Refugee Experience: Forced Migration and Social Networks in Dar Es Salaam, Tanzania," Ph.D. Dissertation, (Anthropology), Graduate School, University of Florida (2003): 102.

6   In this and all future references to our study, I draw on Landau and Jacobsen, "Refugees in the New Johannesburg," and on Karen Jacobsen and Sarah K. Bailey, "Micro-Credit and Banking for Refugees in Johannesburg," in *Forced Migrants in the New Johannesburg: Towards a Local Government Response*, edited by Loren Landau (Johannesburg: Wits University, 2004), 99-102.

7   See also Michela Macchiavello, "Forced Migrants as an Under-Utilized Asset: Refugee Skills, Livelihoods, and Achievements in Kampala, Uganda," (working paper, New Issues in Refugee Research, no. 95, UNHCR, 2003) on Uganda; and Willems, "The Refugee Experience" on Dar es Salaam.

8   USCR, *Pakistan*, 13.

9   USCR, *Pakistan*, 20.

10   Fedde Jan Groot, Deputy Representative to the United Nations High Commissioner for Refugees in South Africa, "UNHCR's Policy on Refugees in Urban Areas: The Case of South Africa," speech at University of the Witwatersrand, Johannesburg, April 30, 2003.

11   Jonathan Bascom, "The New Nomads: An Overview of Involuntary Migration in Africa," in *The Migration Experience in Africa*, ed. J. Baker and R. Aina (Uppsala, Sweden: Nordiska Afrikainstitutet, 1995), 187-219: "relief agencies can ignore urban refugees on the false assumption that if refugees reach a city, they are able to take care of themselves."

12   *UNHCR Resettlement Handbook* (Geneva: UNHCR, November 2004), chap. 5, 6.

13   *UNHCR Resettlement Handbook*, chap. 5, 6.

14   Stefan Sperl, *Evaluation of UNHCR's Policy on Refugees in Urban Areas: A Case Study Review of Cairo*, report for UNHCR Evaluation and Policy Unit, June 2001, 11.

15   Macchiavello, "Forced Migrants," 4.

16   In Uganda, the government allows a small number of registered refugees to settle in Kampala as long as they do not request assistance. This group is made up of professionals and skilled individuals, or of individuals maintained by relatives. In addition, there are an unknown number of self-settled

refugees in Kampala who live there without registering with the Ugandan authorities (Macchiavello, "Forced Migrants," 4).

17   Until 1997, a subsistence allowance was issued to urban Burmese and Afghan refugees in New Delhi; then the allowance was cut off on the grounds of the self-reliance policy. See "Evaluation of UNHCR Policy on Refugees in Urban Areas: A Case Review of New Delhi," UNHCR EPAU, 2002, 20.

18   USCR, *Pakistan*, 22-23.

19   See for example, Gaim Kibreab, "Pulling the Wool Over the Eyes of Strangers: Refugee Deceit and Trickery in Institutionalized Settings," *Journal of Refugee Studies* Vol.14 (1) (2004): 1-26; Tom Kuhlman, *Burden or Boon? A Study of Eritrean Refugees in the Sudan* (Amsterdam: V.U. Uitgeverij, 1990); Willems, "Refugee Experience"; Marc Sommers, *Fear in Bongoland: Burundi Refugees in Urban Tanzania* (New York: Berghahn Books, 2001); Landau and Jacobsen, "Refugees in New Johannesburg," 44-46; J. L. Weaver, "Searching for Survival: Urban Ethiopian Refugees in Sudan," *Journal of Developing Areas,* Vol. 22, No. 4 (1987/88): 457-75; A. Karadawi, "The Problem of Urban Refugees in Sudan," in *Refugees: A Third World Dilemma,* ed. John R. Rogge (New Jersey: Rowman & Littlefield, 1987), 115-129; Jonathan Crush, "The Dark Side of Democracy: Migration, Human Rights and Xenophobia in South Africa," *International Migration* No. 38 (2000): 103-34; Sperl, *Evaluation.*

20   USCR, *Pakistan*, 20.

21   Interviewed by Loren Landau at the Hillbrow Police Station in Johannesburg on July 18, 2003.

22   The following section draws on Eileen Miamidian and Karen Jacobsen, "Livelihood Interventions for Urban Refugees," paper, Alchemy Project Workshop, Maputo, February 19-20, 2004; and Jacobsen and Bailey, "Micro-Credit," 99-102.

23   Willems, "Refugee Experience," 201.

24   Financial needs are widely reported. For example, Afghan and Burmese refugee communities in New Delhi stressed financial difficulties as one of their biggest problems. See *Evaluation of UNHCR Policy on Refugees in Urban Areas: A Case Review of New Delhi,* report for UNHCR Evaluation and Policy Unit, 2000, 20.

25   F. Belvedere, Z. Kimmie, and E. Mogodi, *National Refugee Baseline Survey: Final Report,* Community Agency for Social Enquiry, Japan International Cooperation, and UNHCR 2003, 76.

26   Jacobsen and Bailey, "Micro-Credit," 100.

27   Sperl, *Evaluation.*

28   Statement to Loren Landau at University of Witwatersrand, Johannesburg, March 12, 2004.

Chapter 4

Beyond the Country of First Asylum: Refugees in Third Countries

---

The economic activities of forced migrants provide new perspectives on the global political economy in the twenty-first century. This chapter looks at the transnational links refugees create between their asylum countries and their homeland, particularly through remittances. The chapter begins with a discussion of the "wider diaspora"—those refugees, asylum-seekers, and other migrants from conflict-affected countries, who travel to or are resettled in countries well beyond their home regions. We explore the economic problems experienced by these refugees in third countries, and the added burden of the obligation to send remittances. Does the remittance behavior of refugees differ from that of other migrants? Are refugees more or less likely than other migrants to retain linkages with their families in their countries of origin? This chapter explores how refugees send remittances, and the implications of sending remittances for those who send them, as well as those who receive them.

In earlier chapters, we explored the economic experience of refugees in camps and urban areas in countries of first asylum, that is, those that border their countries of origin. In this chapter, we focus on those who move beyond first asylum countries to more distant third countries[1] of Europe, North America, and Australia, and to the "new" asylum countries, such as South Africa or Poland. These refugees are a part of what Khalid Koser and Nicholas Van Hear call the "wider diaspora," in contrast to the "near diaspora" who live in countries of first asylum.[2] The wider diaspora includes resettled refugees and asylum-seekers as well as migrants from refugee-producing countries who do not apply for asylum, or who arrived in the third country before the conflict began in their home country. In most third countries, this latter group is categorized as economic migrants, but they also contribute to the category of undocumented or illegal migrants who try to operate below the sightline of national authorities. The case of the Somali diaspora is illustrative. Somali migrants are found in a many countries, but because they fall into different categories the exact nature and magnitude of their dispersal is not well known. As Cindy Horst explains, many Somalis migrated before the civil war in Somalia began in 1991, for education or job opportunities, and now hold various types of residence permits or are nationals of their new countries. Then, there are those who fled after the war began: some are still registered as asylum-seekers, others hold temporary permits, others have full refugee status, and some have become nationals of their new countries. In addition, there is a large number of non-registered and illegal migrants.

As a consequence of these multiple categories, says Horst, estimates of the number of Somalis in any third country vary widely. In the UK, estimates range from the official government number (which excludes pre-conflict Somalis) of 20,000 to 100,000. The total Somali diaspora—that is, the number of Somalis who have fled to neighboring countries and beyond—has been estimated at roughly 1.5 million.[3]

In this chapter, we explore the third country experiences of all those who come from refugee-producing countries. Although not all were individually persecuted or targets of violence, most of them had their livelihoods or families destroyed by the protracted conflict in their home countries. In third countries, they experience many of the same economic problems as resettled refugees or asylum-seekers, but face additional problems related to their undocumented legal status or lack of refugee status. We examine their economic experiences, particularly the economic pressures they are under to support their families back in their home countries, and how these obligations are fulfilled through remittances.

The Wider Diaspora: Resettled Refugees, Asylum-Seekers, and Other Migrants in Third Countries

There are two official ways for migrants from refugee-producing countries to gain entry to third countries: as resettled refugees and as asylum-seekers. A third, non-official way is to cross the border illegally, by smuggling or visa fraud. Migrants can also gain entry on short-term visas, such as tourist or student visas, and then over-stay their allotted time, thereby losing their legal status. Given the very small pro-portions of refugees who gain access to third countries through resettlement or formal asylum processes, the third way has become the fastest if most risky route, and poses growing problems for both the migrants themselves and the governments of the destination countries.

Resettled Refugees

Resettlement is the selection and transfer of refugees from a first asylum country to a designated resettlement country, which accords them permanent protection guar-antees, including legal residence, and allows them to integrate in the national com-munity.[4] As envisaged by UNHCR, third country resettlement is one of the "durable solutions" to the refugee predicament because it enables permanent immi-gration. The process of resettlement begins in countries of first asylum with the identification of particular refugees as candidates for resettlement. They are usually those in camps who face protection or health risks, but they must also fit the immi-gration criteria imposed by the resettlement country. There are currently just 29 countries accepting refugees for resettlement[5] and they vary greatly in the number of resettled refugees they will take. Some have quotas, ranging from 70,000 (US) to 25 (Iceland). Others accept resettled refugees on an ad hoc basis. The USA resettles the largest number, averaging some 54,000 a year. Most countries take far fewer;

after the United States, the next largest number is Canada which resettled some 12,000 in 2001, and after that, the numbers drop off quickly: Australia, Denmark, Sweden and Norway each took between 3-4,000, and the rest took just a few hundred or even fewer. However, it is important to note that resettlement data for different countries is difficult to compare since each country takes a different approach.[6]

Each year, the total number of refugees resettled in third countries is just a small fraction of the global refugee population. During 2001, the International Organization for Migration (IOM), which is responsible for the physical transfer of refugees, resettled a total of 87,380 persons, and a further 33,100 refugees were resettled from countries of first asylum under UNHCR auspices. In the ten-year period from 1992-2001, 284,000 refugees were resettled from first asylum countries. In 2001, UNHCR resettled 30,000 refugees, out of a global refugee population of 12 million, and by 2003, this number had dropped to just under 26,000 out of a global refugee population of 17.1 million.[7] Resettlement is thus a possibility for very few refugees. For example, Tanzania, one of the main host countries in Africa, had a refugee population of over 500,000 in 2001. Of these, only 534 refugees—one percent—were resettled in a third country.[8]

Given the narrow quotas, the chance of being resettled is slim, and indeed many people in refugee camps think of resettlement as akin to winning the lottery. The criteria for resettlement vary from one country to another, but in general, UNHCR—which acts as the interlocutor between the resettlement country and the refugees—seeks to use resettlement as a protection measure. Those refugees who are vulnerable to security threats in the camps are chosen first, and families are moved together. Since most refugees in camps are not at risk, most will not be resettled.

While resettlement is a boon for the very small numbers of refugees who achieve it, resettlement programs are very expensive: involving flights for entire families and further resources to help the newcomers integrate in their destination countries. Resettlement programs thus consume a disproportionately large amount of resources given the small number of refugees who ever benefit from them.[9] One problem arising from the desire for resettlement is that many refugees remain in camps, holding out for it, rather than pursuing more feasible options, such as repatriation or local integration.[10] For these reasons, some observers—including this writer—believe that there should be a reallocation and rethinking of resettlement as a durable solution. We return to this debate later on.

Asylum-Seekers

Many migrants from refugee-producing countries travel directly to third countries to apply for asylum, rather than to the countries neighboring their own. These countries are mainly in Europe and the Americas. Between 1980 and 2002, 9.6 million applications for asylum were lodged in thirty-eight countries in Europe, North America, Oceania, and Asia.[11] These include those who will eventually be granted refugee status (in the United States, they are referred to as "asylees"), and those who do not fall under the Convention, but who cannot safely return to their home countries and are in need of international protection. For the latter, also known as "non-Convention" refugees, states grant various forms of so-called "complementary" or temporary protection. Some are treated in the same manner as Convention Refugees and are referred to as de facto refugees, with full rights to permanent residence, and assistance with family reunion and other needs. In other states, those who do not fall under the Convention are accorded secondary status, with fewer rights and limited duration of stay. Still other states merely tolerate their presence, pending eventual deportation, and grant them no rights at all.[12]

According to UNHCR,[13] in 2003, the total number of asylum applications submitted in one hundred and forty-one countries was 807,000, (a decrease from 915,000 reported in 2001). Countries receiving the largest number of new asylum claims during 2003 were France (59,800), Germany (50,600), the United Kingdom (49,400), the United States (43,300), South Africa (35,900), Austria (32,400), Canada (31,900), and Sweden (31,300). In many countries, there is a large backlog of asylum applications, which can remain in the system—sometimes for years. At the end of 2003, the largest number of undecided cases were reported by the United States (335,000), Germany (154,000), South Africa (84,000), the Netherlands (45,000), Canada (42,000), Sweden (35,000), and Austria (32,300). Whereas many countries were able to reduce the number of undecided cases during 2003, increases in the backlog were reported by South Africa (60%), Belgium (13%), Austria (10%) and Sweden (6%).

Resettled refugees and asylum-seekers, together with their co-nationals who have avoided officialdom but are present in a third country through other, sometimes non-legal methods, constitute the refugee component of the "wider diaspora." We turn now to their economic experience.

Refugees' Economic Experience in Third Countries

Whatever their reason for migrating—loss of livelihood or flight from violence and persecution—most migrants and refugees share similar economic experiences after their arrival in third countries. Except for a small elite who manage to come with significant resources, this experience is one of reduced financial means, low income, and high rates of dependence, either on formal assistance (welfare or refugee programs) or on help from friends and family. As immigrants become economically integrated into the labor market, we normally expect their welfare dependence to fall as their income rises, and that they will escape the low-income group. However, this upward mobility does not always occur as expected.[14] For the subset of migrants who are from conflict-affected countries (resettled refugees, asylum-seekers and others), a particular set of factors can retard this process of economic integration. In the remainder of this chapter, we explore these factors, noting that we have relatively little data on the economic experiences of this refugee subset. We do not know how long it takes refugees in third countries to emerge from the poverty they enter after their arrival. While this knowledge is important in and of itself, it would also help us to answer the question of whether resettlement can benefit those left behind—through the remittances sent by resettled refugees.

The Burden of Debt

One of the most significant burdens for new arrivals is the debt many have incurred during the different phases of their flight to third countries. The first phase, internal displacement and flight from their home country, deprives most refugees of their savings and other assets, so that by the time they arrive in the country of first asylum they are already impoverished. During their stay in countries of first asylum, many refugees find ways to pursue livelihoods, as discussed in Chapters Two and Three, but they rarely make enough to accumulate savings or otherwise prepare the household for economic viability in third countries. Finally, the journey to the third country is itself an expensive proposition. Resettled refugees have to borrow the money for their airline tickets from the International Organization of Migration (IOM), and this debt remains with them for years, affecting their credit standing. The IOM debt is small, however, compared with the other costs incurred by asylum-seekers. One set of costs is visas. Another is the fees paid to smugglers or other facilitators. Despite the UNHCR's recommendation that visa requirements should not be imposed on nationals of countries where there are civil wars, generalized violence, or widespread human rights violations, since 1995, the European Union (EU) has adopted binding measures which require nationals of more than one-hundred and thirty states to be in possession of a visa in order to enter the EU. These countries include all the major refugee-generating countries, whose nationals also need a transit visa to travel through the airports of many EU countries. It is not possible to be issued a visa for the purpose of claiming asylum, nor can one apply for asylum at an embassy in one's country of origin.[15] Strict visa regimes, carrier sanctions, and other obstacles to reaching their borders are also in place for the United States, Canada, and Australia, particularly since the events of September 11, 2001.

These obstacles mean there are now few legal routes for those seeking asylum in European or North American countries, and this plays into the hands of human smugglers and traffickers. Many asylum-seekers can only get into third countries by using smugglers, and many arrive indebted—either to the smugglers, or to the asylum seeker's family who raised the money to get them to their destination country. Those migrants who cannot pay the extortionate costs associated with smuggling are sometimes forced into slave labor or criminal activities once they arrive. In 1997, the German Federal Refugee Office estimated that about half their asylum-seekers were smuggled into the country, and in the late 1990s, the Dutch Immigration Service put their estimate higher, at 60-70% of asylum applicants. Interestingly, the groups who are most likely to resort to smugglers (Kosovars, Afghans, and Iraqis) are also those who are statistically most likely to be recognized as genuine refugees.[16] Before they even begin their new lives, refugees newly arrived in third countries carry with them significant debt. Next they must contend with startup expenses and high costs of living, and many must find new ways to borrow—from friends and family already in the third country, or sometimes moneylenders.

Legal Permission to Work

Once inside the asylum country, the first obstacle to finding work is legal status. Resettled refugees, as legal residents, are permitted to work; but in many countries asylum-seekers may not work while the decision to grant them status is being considered. In Europe, the situation varies according to the country in which asylum is sought.[17] Some countries (Denmark, France, Luxembourg, Portugal, UK, and Italy) do not allow asylum-seekers to work legally. Others permit them access to the labor market only after a certain period (3-12 months), or subject to certain conditions; for example, after first obtaining a special permit, or by proving that their job cannot be filled by an EU citizen. The reason for this policy is, apparently, to discourage would-be asylum-seekers from relocating for economic reasons—that is, primarily under the incentive of employment. However, the European Council on Refugees and Exiles (ECRE) says the significance of the right to work is often exaggerated as a "pull-factor." Given the ease with which illegal migrants find work on the black market in many western countries, it is unlikely that those whose sole motivation is to find work would bother to make an asylum claim, thereby attracting the attention of the authorities.[18]

Should asylum-seekers be allowed to work? Many are genuine refugees who will eventually be allowed to remain, once the government's status determination procedures have occurred. Being able to seek employment early on will help their eventual integration into their host society. Since many asylum-seekers are highly skilled, they can fill shortages in the domestic workforce; and if given the ability to support themselves, migrants will not be a drain on public resources. In addition, it is worth remembering that the right to work is stated in Article 17 of the 1951 UN Convention on Refugees, which all of the European and North American countries have signed.

Labor Market Obstacles

Compared with natives, migrants—especially those from non-western countries—face greater difficulties finding formal employment. Blume shows that in Denmark, the rate of participation in the work force among male immigrants from non-western countries is much lower than it is for natives, and so is the *employment rate*: 80% for male natives vs. below 40% for male immigrants from non-western countries. Welfare dependence is still high after many years in the host country.[19] Similarly, we found in our Johannesburg survey that one third of our South African respondents reported working full time in either the formal or informal sector, compared with only seven percent of migrant respondents. Of those respondents in our sample who were working, over a quarter (twenty-eight percent) of the migrants claimed to be self-employed, compared with six percent of the South Africans. When immigrants are able to find employment, they are often paid less than what natives receive for comparable work.[20]

Migrants' low employment and participation rates reflect a range of difficulties and obstacles. For potential employers, even those who do not suffer from anti-foreigner prejudice and xenophobia, hiring a migrant or a refugee can lead to all kinds of problems. The employer may be unfamiliar with the legal right of refugees to work, and may not wish to take the chance. The refugee himself may have difficulty establishing proof of the validity of his job training, certification, and educational qualifications. Language or accent skills are often a problem, particularly for certain kinds of work. While all migrants face these obstacles, refugees have a particular set of advantages and disadvantages. On the one hand, refugees' flight experience can result in particular mental and physical health problems or needs that will inhibit economic participation. Also, refugees may place a priority on tracing or becoming reunited with family members from whom they were separated during their flight. Many refugees seek to address these needs first, before advancing their economic integration into their new society. On the other hand, in more progressive third countries, resettled refugees and asylees are at an advantage compared with other migrants, because they have access to state assistance programs—such as trauma counseling,[21] job training, and re-certification—which can speed up their economic participation. In the EU, there is wide variation among the member states in the help given to recognized refugees; and for many, these difficulties must be faced alone or with the help only of family and friends. Some countries provide special packages of financial assistance and advice lasting several years, while others provide only brief integration programs or make no special provisions at all.

The Burden of Sending Remittances

Refugees in third countries have double economic obligations: to the family they left behind, in countries of origin or in refugee camps, and to their own households with them in the third country.[22] The obligation to the family left behind is met through remittances, usually in the form of cash transfers, but also through other economic contributions made on behalf of people at home—such as payment for overseas education or for migration abroad. The latter are not technically recorded as remittances since they are not actually transferred to the sending country but they constitute outlays by the refugee in the form of payments for tickets, migration agents, documents, accommodation, and other costs incurred during and after travel.

While the family abroad benefits from remittances, the effect on the sender can be a serious economic setback.[23] Resettled refugees and asylum-seekers are among the poorest of immigrants, in unstable financial situations and with very little discretionary income. Sending remittances can mean they are not able to make human capital investments, such as improving their language skills, or gaining work skills and education in their new country. Sending remittances can prevent debt repayments (such as the IOM debt) and can create a poverty trap that decreases or slows their chances of improving their situations. Without savings, the slightest set-back—a car needing repairs, an unexpected hospital bill, a reduction in work hours—can trigger a financial crisis. In her study of resettled Sudanese refugees in Cairo and San Diego, California, Stephanie Riak Akuei says the following about the refugees' experiences with sending remittances:

> newcomers arrive rather optimistic about supporting relatives left behind. In their optimism and lack of knowledge about the hurdles that are to fol-low many refugees...devote sizeable portions (ca. $100-300/month) of their cash allowances received during the first few months to remittances. They also incur huge bills resulting from the numerous and long phone calls they make—unknowingly at higher rates—to relatives and friends they have been separated from and miss. Over time, anxieties build when people find they lack enough money to cover their own expenses while try-ing to juggle these with the needs of loved ones whose circumstances they see as much worse than their own.[24]

We can infer both from the level of flows of remittances back to regions of ori-gin, and from anecdotal reports, that remittance sending is a well-established prac-tice of refugees in third countries. However, there is little research on the remittance-sending behavior of refugees in the west or the economic impact on them. Whether the financial burden of sending remittances affects refugees' attain-ment of self-sufficiency or economic integration is only beginning to be explored.

Flows of Refugee Remittances

As we have seen in earlier chapters, receiving remittances makes an important dif-ference in the survival of displaced households both in countries of origin and in countries of first asylum. Refugee remittances enable families to survive during con-flict and displacement, and since some portion of remittances also goes to religious organizations and hometown associations, they also sustain communities in crisis.[25] In conflict-affected countries like Sri Lanka and Somalia, remittances constitute the primary financial sector and most important source of national revenue. In Sri Lanka, remittances have grown from around USD150 million in 1980 to about USD1 billion in 2000, and have eclipsed official development assistance and humanitarian aid.[26] In Somalia and Somaliland, remittances from both labor migrants and refugees are estimated at between USD500 million and USD1 billion annually, and constitute that region's largest source of earnings, more than 10 times larger than receipts of foreign aid.[27] Making estimates is complicated by differences in accounting at the national level, accuracy of reporting and definition, and by the varying ability of national agencies to track all monies sent. Estimates of remittance amounts vary considerably; some argue that these numbers are underestimated by as much as 25%. At the household level, information about remittance inflows is difficult to obtain, for the same reasons that it is difficult to get full information about household income. Like most people, refugees and migrants tend to under-report income, either because they don't include certain categories, or because they don't wish to reveal all sources. This might explain why, for example, ninety-four percent of Afghan refugees interviewed by UNHCR stated that they did not receive remittances from abroad.[28] Even taking underreporting into account, the proportion of the refugee population in first asylum countries that receives remittances is small. Most refugees are not fortunate enough to have relative abroad.

Refugees in third countries transfer remittances in various ways, often using agents or traders who are quicker and cheaper than banks or Western Union, or through informal channels, such as the Sri Lankans' *undial* system, or the *xawilaad* system used by Somalis. Many of these organizations have been affected by the consequences of the terrorist attacks on the United States in 2001. The U.S. Patriot Act, for example, required organizations transmitting money to enhance their technologies and increase their compliance, and some were shut down by the U.S. government, which claimed they financed terrorism.[29] These actions have increased the burden on remittance senders, who must struggle to find alternate transfer means, many of which have increased their fees.

Pressures to Remit

Given the financial drain and the obstacles to their economic advancement posed by sending remittances, why do refugees do so? Remittance obligation exists for migrants from all countries, but for refugees in third countries, these obligations may be stronger because their families back home are not only living in poverty, as are most migrants', but are more likely to be displaced or in danger. This places an even greater obligation on those family members who have escaped and made it to a wealthy country. There is the knowledge that families "back home" need money, either for daily subsistence needs, such as health care, housing, and children's education, or to pay off debts, including those arising from outlays to send the asylum seeker abroad. Cindy Horst interviewed a Somali refugee in Minneapolis who said the one-hundred and fifty dollars she sends to her brother in Kakuma refugee camp and the one-hundred and fifty dollars she sends to relatives in Somalia "are part of her monthly bill" and she always pays them before even paying the rent: "If I cannot pay the rent, I will still manage. But if those people do not get the money I send them, life will be too tough for them."[30]

Resettled refugees and asylum-seekers who "make it out" have often been financially assisted by their family, either at home or elsewhere in the diaspora. This support is sometimes part of a broader household survival strategy, in which the refugee "scout" is an investment who will lead to both to future income (in the form of remittances) and possibly even resettlement for the entire household. These scouts are under great pressure from their families. In her study of Sudanese Dinka urban refugees in Cairo, Riak Akuei found:

> When Dinka refugees depart from Cairo, they are sent off with heavy "cultural" reminders and directives. Songs and formally spoken words relay messages intended to remind people that in the forthcoming sea of opportunities and options that await them, they should not forget who they are and what it means to be a Dinka (*Yin ee Muonyjiang!*). Among other morsels of advice, expectations are conveyed to those taking leave that they should not forget their responsibilities and obligations to help their people back home and elsewhere who are suffering."[31]

Resettled refugees in third countries can become responsible for large numbers of people from their extended families in various locations.[32] In Riak Akuei's study, one head of household of a Dinka family in San Diego became directly responsible for twenty-four male and female extended family members, and indirectly, sixty-two persons total within the first two years of resettlement. The family members were in Cairo; Kakuma Refugee Camp, Kenya; Kampala, Khartoum, Nairobi, Tripoli, and other parts of Sudan.[33] Remittance pressure is not necessarily imposed on refugees as soon as they make it to a prosperous country. A refugee will be given time to become economically established first. Indeed, the flow of resources may continue from families to the refugee scout for some time beyond the arrival period. But as time passes, and the refugee's family considers that she has had enough time to get established, the pressure to remit will be on.

The power of refugees' family obligations comes from more than a sense of duty; other motivating factors may include notions of family dignity and pride. A refugee scout knows that she cannot shirk her responsibilities to her family back home on pain of ostracization, and of bringing shame to her family. The diaspora network is far-flung and likely to be present in the country where the refugee scout settles; thus, there is no escaping its watchful eye, unless she changes her identity or cuts all contact with the network (which some do, at great cost). Like economic migrants, refugees desire to retain contact, increase their social status, and preserve their dignity before the gaze of their community—whether this community is part of the diaspora or in the country of origin. This community notices who sends and who does not, and remittances are a way to exhibit connections, prove that relatives are cared for, and maintain contact with the country of origin. Studies of African refugees in the United States, including Sudanese refugees resettled from Egypt in San Diego and Somalis in Minneapolis, suggest that it is a matter of honor for the refugees to send a portion of their earnings back to their next-of-kin once they have found a job.[34] While much of this money goes to meet basic subsistence needs, it is also utilized to pay for marriage ceremonies and other social needs, and remittances pay for the migration of relatives left behind. The author's own preliminary research with resettled African refugees and asylum-seekers in the New England area reveals a widespread desire to send money back to their families. In interviews with Liberian, Sudanese, and Congolese refugees in Boston and Manchester, New Hampshire, men and women spoke repeatedly of their fervent wish to help their families, and the anguish they feel at not being able to send more. But they also lamented the difficulty of finding extra money, given the economic strains they were under trying to adapt to their new lives, find work, and provide for their children. Sending remittances can create personal and social problems too. Cindy Horst tells of one Somali refugee in Minneapolis who sent five-hundred dollars to the Kenyan refugee camps and two-hundred to relatives in Somalia every month, and who felt that as long as he has that responsibility, he cannot marry; as this would create new responsibilities that would interfere with his ability to support his family abroad.[35]

Sending remittances also contributes to a risk-reduction strategy for both refugees and their families left behind in conflict-affected countries. Placing a person abroad, who might help out when there are difficult times in the country of origin, serves to increase the reach of the family's safety net. For the refugee, uncertainty in the outcome of the migratory experience—including the asylum application—means that remittances serve as insurance that there is still a place within the family if the immigrant needs to return home. This motive might be especially important for asylum-seekers who are at risk of deportation.[36]

Do Remittances Justify Resettlement?

More knowledge and understanding about refugee remittance patterns and behavior will help us address an interesting debate that has arisen about resettlement. The level of international aid resources assigned in resettlement is often criticized because it is disproportionate to the relatively small number of refugees who ever get resettled. In addition, the promise of resettlement raises problems for refugees in camps and urban areas in countries of first asylum, because it can act as a pull factor for refugees and a disincentive for integration or repatriation. The counter argument is that resettlement is often the only option for refugees in protracted situations, and after resettlement they are in a position to contribute to the economic well-being of their kin back home by virtue of the remittances they send. In Cairo, Sperl says, local integration is not possible, nor does UNHCR have the funds to provide adequate support locally, and resettlement is the only concrete solution.

> In addition, the formation of strong diaspora communities in countries of resettlement is a significant element...Not only do these communities create...a home away from home for the displaced by providing cultural and religious continuity and a social support network, but they have also become an important source of financial support for those left behind in countries of first asylum and origin.[37]

Sperl found that in Cairo the number of refugees receiving remittances from relatives abroad appears to have risen in line with the increased resettlement departures. However, he adds that much support also comes from relatives in the Gulf countries, which implies that it is migrant workers, not resettled refugees, who send the funds. While resettled refugees could potentially be a source of support for their kin left behind, and often are, so far there is relatively little evidence to show that their contribution outweighs the significant burden it imposes. The burden of remittances on resettled refugees and asylum-seekers in third countries can create a "remittance trap" that prevents them from establishing an economic foothold and keeps them in poverty. However, there is no question that for those left behind who benefit from these transfers, they are a life-saving factor. This leaves the question of how best to create a system of resettlement and asylum in third countries that assists those in need, but does not at the same time lead to the creation of unsupportable economic burdens on those who must try to establish their livelihoods in third countries. While the wider diaspora of refugees plays an important role in the survival of their relatives living in the sending region, the obligation to send money is a real burden to their own economic survival. In order to reduce this burden, many refugees in third countries encourage their relatives to invest in individual or communal enterprises that will lead to self-sufficiency, rather than to consume the remittances. Alternatively, they try to enable their relatives to migrate, either to join them in the third country, or to another third country.[38]

What kind of policy initiatives would benefit the refugees, their families left behind, and the management of migration? Many have suggested that in migration contexts, remittance-senders should be seen as agents of development for their countries of origin. This is particularly the case for refugees, whose home countries are in particularly bad shape, and whose relatives there and in the neighboring countries where they are displaced must survive with few resources. Refugee policies and relief assistance would do well to incorporate the fact of remittance sending into their understanding of how best to help refugees, especially those who are the senders.[39]

Notes

1   The country of origin is the first country; the country over the border to which refugees initially flee is the second (or first country of asylum), and the country to which they move after that is the third country.

2   Koser and Van Hear, "Asylum Migration," 1.

3   Cindy Horst, "Money and Mobility: Transnational Livelihood Strategies of the Somali Diaspora," *Global Migration Perspectives*, No. 9, October 2004.

4   This definition is taken from www.more.fi/. See also UNHCR's definition at www.unhcr.ch/cgi-bin/texis/vtx/home?page=PROTECT&id=3b8366bc4&ID=3b8366bc4&PUBLISHER=TWO

5   For a useful discussion of the resettlement countries' approaches and for data on resettlement, see George Wright, "ICAR Navigation Guide: Resettlement Programmes," Information Centre about Asylum and Refugees in the UK (London: Kings College, 2003); available at www.icar.org.uk/content/res/nav/keyiss.html.

6   Wright says quotas are only countries' resettlement forecasts for the coming year. The actual number of refugees resettled might stray below or above the

forecast. Some states are more flexible about the manner in which numbers of actual arrivals may deviate from their initial quotas. See Wright, "ICAR Navigation Guide."

7   UNHCR, "Global Refugee Trends: Overview of Refugee Populations, New Arrivals, Durable Solutions, Asylum-Seekers and Other Persons of Concern to UNHCR," 2004; available at www.unhcr.ch/cgi-bin/texis/vtx/statistics.

8   Willems, "Refugee Experience," 102, (citing UNHCR statistics).

9   In the United States, each year the Congress passes Omnibus Appropriations legislation, which sets funding levels for overseas refugee assistance and the U.S. refugee resettlement program. For FY2005, the Office of Refugee Resettlement (ORR), which is a domestic program and part of the Dept. of Human Services, experienced the largest increase in its overall budget since 1999, with a total appropriation of $488 million, which will be cut slightly by an overall rescission to $484 million. By contrast, funding for the State Department, which is responsible for the U.S. government's overseas refugee programs, was set at $770 million for the Migration and Refugee Assistance (MRA) account. However, this account includes funding for the reception and placement of resettled refugees, and $30 million for the Emergency Refugee and Migration Assistance (ERMA) Fund. This funding was to support the President's goal of admitting 70,000 refugees to the United States in 2005.

10   Tom Kuhlman, "Organized Versus Spontaneous Settlement of Refugees in Africa," in *African Refugees: Development Aid and Repatriation*, ed. Howard Adelman and John Sorenson (Boulder, CO: Westview Press, 1994), 117-142.

11   UNHCR, "Global Refugee Trends" and also www.migration information.org/DataTools/asylum.cfm.

12   For more details and statistics on asylum in Europe, see www.ecre.org/fact file/facts.shtml.

13   The following statistics are all taken from UNHCR, "Global Refugee Trends."

14   Karen Blume, "Immigrants and Low-Income in Denmark—Is Self-employment Associated with an Upward Income Mobility?" (WIDER Conference on Poverty, International Migration and Asylum, September 27-28, 2002); available at www.wider.unu.edu/conference/conference-2002-3/conference-2002-3-papers.htm

15   The possibility of humanitarian visas and applying for asylum at embassies is currently under debate in the EU. For more details, see www.ecre.org/fact file/facts.shtml.

16   John Morrison and Beth Crosland, "The Trafficking and Smuggling of Refugees: The End Game in European Asylum Policy?" (working paper, New Issues in Refugee Research, no. 39, UNHCR, 2001), 17.

17   For a discussion of social and economic rights standards for non-nationals in Europe, see John A. Dent, "Research Paper on the Social and Economic Rights of Non-Nationals in Europe," European Council on Refugees and Exiles (ECRE) Commissioned Research Paper (2002); available at www.ecre.org/research/socecon.pdf.

18   See ECRE's Web site containing asylum statistics at www.ecre.org/factfile/facts.shtml#12.

19   Blume, "Immigrants," 2.

20   Loren Landau and Karen Jacobsen, "Refugees in the New Johannesburg," *Forced Migration Review*, 19, January 2004.

21   For a review of these programs and interventions, see Carola Eyber, FMO Research Guide: Psychosocial Issues (October 2002). Forced Migration Online; available at www.forcedmigration.org/guides/fmo004/.

22   For more on remittances see Khalid Koser and Nadje Al-Ali, eds., *New Approaches to Migration? Transnational Communities and the Transformation of Home* (London: Routledge. 2001); Horst, "Money"; Nicholas Van Hear, "'I Went as Far as My Money Would Take Me': Conflict, Forced Migration and Class," (8th IASFM Conference, Chiang Mai, Thailand, January 2003).

23   The author wishes to acknowledge her student, David Sussman, whose thesis work contributed to this section. See David D. Sussman, "The Impact of Remitting upon the Self-Sufficiency of Immigrants in Boston," M.A.L.D. Thesis, Fletcher School of Law and Diplomacy, Tufts University, May 2004.

24   Stephanie Riak Akuei, *Remittances as Unforeseen Burdens: Considering Displacement, Family, and Resettlement Contexts in Refugee Livelihood and Well Being. Is There Anything States or Organisations Can Do?* UNHCR Evaluation and Policy Unit Background Document (May 2004); available at www.unhcr.ch/.

25   In post-conflict countries, like El Salvador and Rwanda, there is evidence that remittances allow households to supplement earned income or subsistence production, and raise income levels above the national poverty line. See Sarah Gammage and Jorge Fernandez, "Conflict, Displacement and Reintegration: Household Survey Evidence from El Salvador," (working paper, New Issues in Refugee Research, no. 25, UNHCR, 2000), 22. In Afghanistan, Sue Lautze's study found that remittances have played an important role in the economic survival of communities. Sue Lautze et al., "Qaht-E-Pool 'A Cash Famine': Food Insecurity in Afghanistan 1999-2002," (2002); available at famine.tufts.edu/pdf/cash_famine.pdf.

26   Van Hear, "'I Went as Far,'" 9-10. See also Peter Gammeltoft, "Remittances and Other Financial Flows to Developing Countries," *Migration-Development Links: Evidence and Policy Options* Paper for the Migration-Development Links Project at the Danish Institute for International Studies,

Copenhagen (2002); available at www.cdr.dk/ResTHEMES/conflict/migdev final.htm.

27   Ismail Ahmed, "Remittances and Their Economic Impact in Post-war Soma-liland," *Disasters* 24 (2000): 380-38.

28   Melissa Phillips, "The Role and Impact of Humanitarian Assets in Refugee-hosting Countries," (working paper, New Issues in Refugee Research, no. 84, UNHCR, 2003),13.

29   One of these was Al Barakaat, which once sent some $380,000 a day, adding up to $140 million annually. Overseas Somalis were obliged to find other institutions for sending. Al Barakaat's competitor, Dahab Shiil, has increased from as much as $70,000 to $170,000 daily. Horst and Van Hear, "Counting the Cost," 32.

30   Horst, "Money," 12.

31   Akuei, "Remittances," 2.

32   Horst, "Money," 2.

33   Akuei, "Remittances," 3.

34   See Akuei, "Remittances"; Sperl, *Evaluation*; and Horst, "Money."

35   Horst, "Money," 12.

36   Sussman, "Impact."

37   Sperl, *Evaluation*, 32.

38   Horst, "Money," 15.

39   For more on linking development and migration policies, see others mentioned in this chapter and Nina Nyberg Sørensen, "The Development Dimension of Migrant Remittances," (Migration Policy Research Working Paper Series, no. 1, IOM, 2004).

Chapter 5

Can Humanitarian Programs Support the Livelihoods of the Displaced?

I n earlier chapters, we explored how once an emergency has passed, refugees struggle to re-establish their livelihoods in camps and urban areas, in countries of first asylum and in third countries. In the face of declining humanitarian assistance, including food aid, refugees in protracted situations do their best to sustain themselves and their families by pursing economic activities. The problem of how to assist these refugees is one of the unmet challenges facing the international refugee regime.[1] This chapter explores some ways in which aid agencies have supported refugees' livelihood efforts. Not everyone agrees on the wisdom of humanitarian agencies becoming involved in supporting the livelihoods of refugees. Strict interpreters of the traditional humanitarian position argue that supporting livelihoods goes beyond the humanitarian imperative, which is to save lives and to prevent suffering for those affected by violent conflict and war. However, most humanitarian agencies take a more open position, arguing that enabling livelihoods can also save lives and prevent suffering.

It is likely that refugees would be able to support themselves and their families in host countries *if they were able to exercise their rights to work, move around freely, and practice their professions.* Even more refugees would be able to support themselves if they had access to productive land. Therefore, one of the most important advocacy initiatives on the part of donor countries and humanitarian agencies, especially UNHCR, is to move host governments towards a more rights-positive position that would allow refugees to be economically active. In countries where refugees have been able to exercise these rights, such as Côte d'Ivoire in the 1990s, they have had relative economic success and have benefited their host countries.

However, as discussed in earlier chapters, most host governments are moving in the opposite direction. For a variety of reasons—security concerns, host fatigue, economic pressures—governments are increasingly reluctant to allow refugees to pursue economic activities outside of camps or designated zones. Aid agencies therefore operate within narrow policy confines, trying to support refugees' economic activities without crossing legal boundaries or contravening national policy. This usually means that in first asylum countries, refugees can only be assisted in camps; in urban areas they are on their own.

The more progressive aid agencies recognize that refugees are agents capable of improving their own economic and social situation, and that with or without international assistance they develop their own livelihood and survival strategies. These agencies try to use program interventions that support and build on that capacity, rather than simply providing assistance or doing things for refugees that they are capable of doing themselves.[2] The challenge is how to do this effectively in protracted refugee situations. During emergencies, UNHCR and its implementing NGOs can mobilize effectively—mortality rates are quickly reduced and refugees' urgent needs are met. But once the emergency has passed, (that is, high inflows have slowed, mortality rates have declined, and the camp has stabilized), what follows is the "care and maintenance" phase. Many see this phase as a form of "warehousing," in which refugees are parked in camps and provided with most of their basic needs until the hoped-for repatriation happens. If their situations become protracted and repatriation does not happen, there is no vision of how refugees could become an asset to host countries, or how to allow them to promote economic development.[3] This failure to look for more creative and positive approaches represents an extraordinary waste of resources. As a UNHCR officer once remarked, "It doesn't make sense to confine refugees to camps and to insist that they survive on food aid when agricultural and income-generating opportunities are waiting to be exploited."[4]

Enabling Livelihoods: The Need for Credit

As food rations and other humanitarian support are reduced in protracted situations, refugees must find ways to support themselves and their families. Cash is needed to buy the things that aren't adequately provided by assistance programs, or that are cut when aid is reduced. These things include firewood, transportation, bribes, and school and hospital fees. Figuring out how to generate income becomes an all-consuming activity. Most refugees in rural hosting areas have been farmers or engaged in other primary production (fishing, livestock) in their home countries, and they continue to try to pursue these kinds of livelihoods in camps. NGOs support them by providing tools, seeds, and extension services. However, lack of access to land, restrictions on movement and work, and shortages of production inputs like fertilizer or animal medicine mean that refugees are rarely able to fully exploit opportunities for crop and animal production, fishing, or other potential sources of food and income. Since there is little employment available, most refugees rely on small enterprises based on petty trade or service provision (barbers, food makers, artisans, translators) to generate income. This shift into the informal sector is widespread, and in urban areas, it is the only source of income for most refugees.

One of the most pressing needs in starting a small enterprise is access to credit, and for refugees, there are few sources. In camps, there are no banks, and in urban areas refugees are often unable to use formal banking and credit institutions. In some situations, refugees form self-help groups, known as rotating savings and credit associations (ROSCAs). For a few lucky ones, remittances are an important source of cash. Moneylenders offer credit—but often at exorbitant rates that undermine the possibility of making an enterprise viable. Many people are so desperate they will resort to illicit sources, or illegitimate and dangerous livelihood strategies. For the displaced, lack of access to fair and sufficient credit is a major constraint in the pursuit of sustainable and dignified livelihoods. Is the provision of credit something humanitarian agencies should provide?

The problems associated with introducing humanitarian aid resources into war zones are now well documented and explored.[5] In a displaced community, be it in a refugee camp or an urban setting, humanitarian assistance that seeks to support the livelihoods and economic activities of refugees is no less complicated. In situations where refugees live among local people, in urban or rural areas, aid agencies worry about local resentment and xenophobia when only refugees—and not the impoverished surrounding community—receive assistance. Even in camps, where refugees are separated from the local poor, it is difficult to justify providing refugees with assistance when the host population living outside the camp is as afflicted economically, and is sometimes in even worse straits. For example, in Kakuma camp in north-western Kenya on the border of Sudan, the Sudanese and other refugees living there are, in many ways, better off than the local Turkana population, which has been sidelined from the aid economy. The refugees have access to food, health services, schools, and income generating projects. Even their life chances are more promising—a small proportion of refugees will be resettled in countries in the West, but no Turkana ever will. Whereas it is possible to justify providing traditional relief like food aid to refugees in camps, it is more difficult to justify providing livelihood assistance like microcredit to refugees and not to the local community. Since refugees have to interact with the local community to pursue livelihoods, local resentment is highly counterproductive. In Kakuma camp, the local Turkana population has vented frustrations with the refugees living there by instigating violence against them.[6]

To counter this problem, some agencies, including UNHCR, seek to include the local population in their programs, giving them access to health care, education and clean water.[7] For example, in Uganda, as Tania Kaiser writes:

> the Refugee Affected Area approach has been taken very seriously…it is estimated that forty per cent of the assistance provided by UNHCR in Kibanda has been directed to the area surrounding the settlement in order to facilitate a general improvement in living conditions there and to mitigate possible resentment of the refugees by the Ugandan population.[8]

In searching for ways to help refugees, the difficulty is not simply about the best kinds of programs, but also about finding solutions that are acceptable to host countries in the current climate of restrictive asylum, and with introducing resources intended to benefit refugees into very poor host communities. Without the host country's acquiescence and active involvement, it is difficult for aid agencies to help refugees pursue livelihoods because governments can impose a variety of obstacles to economic activities. Therefore, in designing programs, it is as important to focus on the needs and constraints of host countries (both the government and the citizens) as on those of refugees.

There are two possible ways to support displaced people's livelihoods when they do not have employment. One is by providing funds in the form of loans or grants specifically intended to enable people engage in income earning activities (such as farming, pastoralism, small businesses, trade, etc.) or to seek education and training that will later enable them to engage in the economic realm at a higher level. These economic activities enable people to provide for their households needs through their own efforts. A second way is for an external organization (the state or humanitarian agencies) to provide free services like health care, education, and food aid, so that people do not need a form of employment to support themselves and their households. In the humanitarian sector today, funds are much less likely to be used for income-generating endeavors than for providing free services. Refugees are provided with "free" humanitarian services; they are not generally able to access direct funds (wages or credit) that could enable them to pursue livelihoods on their own. This model is by now well entrenched, and for years it was rarely questioned. Any suggestion that refugees could and should be enabled to support themselves—rather than being obliged to be dependent on humanitarian aid—was countered by the valid argument that in most host countries refugees are not permitted to work or move around freely; and therefore, there is no choice but to provide for their needs while they sit in camps, waiting to return home or be resettled elsewhere. In addition, aid agencies were caught up in their own political economies of aid, and the idea of re-tooling the aid industry so as to move away from the provision of emergency-based services was a task that no agency leaders wanted to take on.

In recent years, however, as protracted situations drag on, levels of humanitarian aid and assistance diminish, and aid agencies can no longer support all the needs of people in refugee camps. Aid agencies are now beginning to recognize the importance of supporting the efforts of displaced people to support themselves. Various experiments and pilot projects are being attempted, such as cash voucher programs, microcredit for refugees, and various income-generating or cash-for-work programs. Often, these are the first programs to be cut, and in general they are not yet well resourced, understood, or evaluated. Moreover, when funded, they are often of poor quality, since it is difficult for relief agency personnel to implement effective livelihood programs. However, a number of NGOs have made real progress in sorting out the difficulties in many non-traditional approaches.

The rest of this chapter explores some of the methods used by local and international aid agencies to promote refugee livelihoods, as opposed to traditional relief programs based on handouts. We begin with UNHCR and its recent efforts to enable self-reliance by encouraging governments to allow refugees to be economically active. Then we explore income-generating activities on the part of international and local NGOs, using case studies. These interventions support livelihoods through microfinance, income-generating projects, vocational training, food for work, and so forth. We also examine the potential negative consequences of various livelihood interventions, how agencies attempt to manage these risks, and how to assess whether such programs have an overall negative or positive outcome.

UNHCR, Refugee Livelihoods, and Self-Reliance

Humanitarian assistance for refugees is normally managed by UNHCR through implementing or operational partners, usually NGOs with experience in sectors like health, education, water and sanitation, and other camp requirements. UNHCR itself is usually not operational in the field; that is, it does not implement assistance programs, but is responsible for selecting, supervising, and monitoring the NGOs it subcontracts in the field. The kinds of programs that support refugee livelihoods usually fall within UNHCR's Community Services. According to UNHCR, Community Services are distinguished from other assistance activities by "the focus on improving the refugees own capacity to meet their needs and solve their own problems."[9]

During much of the 1990s, UNHCR was largely pre-occupied with repatriation and the reintegration of returnees in countries of origin. Since about 2000, UNHCR has demonstrated a new interest in protracted refugee situations, refugee livelihoods, and self–reliance. According to UNHCR's Web site,[10] this development has been the result of several factors that have emerged in the past few years. First, its involvement in fewer large-scale emergency operations and repatriation programs has enabled UNHCR to focus on other forms of relief. Second, declining levels of aid, especially in Africa, mean that over the long term, UNHCR will not be able to continue to meet minimum humanitarian standards by using their current assistance programs. At the same time, donor states and other actors have become increasingly interested in strategies that might lead to a reduction in the levels of relief expenditures. Third, increasing resistance on the part of host states and societies to the long-term presence of refugees on their territory[11] has prompted UNHCR to try to emphasize the positive aspects of refugees, especially their "productive potential."

One of the difficulties UNHCR faces in protracted situations is diminished donor interest in funding refugee assistance programs. The longer the refugees are in a host country, the more inclined contributors are to reduce their funding. In some cases, donors request that UNHCR coordinate its refugee program with ongoing development projects in the area, so that both refugees and nationals benefit. Host governments are also likely to want their nationals to be included in long-term plans, although in most cases, they do not want to allow refugees to become citizens, or to integrate them more fully into their society.

Given these shifts and new sources of pressure, UNHCR has sought to promote "self-reliance" programs for refugees. The guiding philosophy of the self-reliance strategy can be explained as follows: refugees have the skills and potential to stand on their own and build their self-esteem (damaged by the very fact that they are refugees). Moreover, as it is agreed that they will not remain in exile for ever, it is important that they should be prepared for repatriation by being provided with skills and knowledge that will serve them in the reconstruction of their home country. The strategy also aims at creating sustainable structures that can be left in place once the refugees return home. Of equal importance, is the consideration that UNHCR was never designed to be a permanent development agency or to run a kind of parallel system of services for "its" refugees.[12]

Uganda's Self-Reliance Strategy

Programs supporting self-reliance strategies have been tried most successffully in Uganda, as well as in Guinea, Ghana, and Zambia.[13] The long-term assistance strategy for refugees known as "From Local-Settlement to Self-Reliance," was adopted in Uganda in 1999. Designed jointly by the Ugandan government (the Office of the Prime Minister) and UNHCR Uganda, it was intended to enable refugees, particularly the Sudanese living in the West Nile region, to manage their own lives and share services with Ugandan nationals. The Self-Reliance Strategy was to unfold over a transition period of four years.[14] The strategy envisaged eventual repatriation, rather than full integration, as the "durable solution"; that is, citizenship for refugees was not a goal. The objective was that by the year 2003, the refugees would be able to grow or buy their own food, access and pay for basic services, and maintain self-sustaining community structures. UNHCR would continue to be responsible for international protection of refugees and would pursue some legal issues, such as freedom of movement, taxation, trade and employment opportunities for refugees, and temporary access to land. The central government would continue to have overall responsibility for national refugee law and policy. But the plans also addressed the development needs of the socio-economically-marginalized region of northern Uganda hosting most of the refugees. The strategy sought to "find ways to integrate the services provided to the refugees into regular government structures and policies," and to "improve the standard of living of the people in Moyo, Arua, and Adjumani districts, including the refugees."

From the start, the Self-Reliance Strategy (SRS) had promise for a number of reasons. First, the refugees in northwestern Uganda were generally welcomed by the local community, which is of the same ethnicity and shares the same traditions, language, and culture. In this region, the border between Uganda and Sudan represents only an administrative division, and not a real barrier. Moreover, many in the Ugandan host population had themselves been refugees in southern Sudan during the civil wars in Uganda, so there was a sense of reciprocity and a debt of gratitude. This "welcome factor" was seen as an asset in promoting self-reliance. Second, the policy had strong support from the government, and was based at a high level—the Prime Minister's Office. Third, Uganda's existing refugee policy of local settlement allowed and enabled refugees to have access to arable land, and they were already farming.

A perennial problem faced by international agencies trying to support refugees in protracted situations, is the roadblock posed by the "mandates" of other UN agencies. In UN parlance, responsibility for different aspects of development is divided among agencies as follows: UNICEF looks after children, the World Health Organization (WHO) is for health, The UN Population Fund (UNFPA) for reproductive health, UNDP for private sector development, World Bank for post-conflict reconstruction, and so on. Refugees are not seen as falling under "development"—they are part of humanitarian or relief efforts, and utilize different funding structures, namely UNHCR. Development agencies and donors are often reluctant to use their funds for humanitarian purposes, although they do sometimes have programs that include refugees, especially when they are a large percentage of the resident population.

In pursuing the Self-Reliance Strategy in Uganda, UNHCR and the government had to solicit the support of various donor agencies (such as the World Bank, the EU, the Dutch Government, or USAID), and persuade them that maintaining and improving health, education, and income-earning in refugee-hosting areas in the West Nile region was development, and not relief. UNHCR and the government perceived that promoting self-reliance and integrating refugee assistance into national systems of service-delivery would require a change of attitude on the part of all stakeholders involved. As stated in the Strategy paper by UNHCR and the Ugandan government:[15]

> **Refugees** need to learn to give up unrealistic expectations and demands for continuous external support from the international community and UNHCR in particular. They will be further sensitized to take responsibility for themselves and their communities (including tax payments and payment of school and health fees).

> **UNHCR and NGOs** need to move away from "relief thinking" and parallel service delivery to facilitate self-help initiatives and adopt an integrated approach with the district. International NGOs and implementing partners [will] be expected to phase out once local systems for delivery are able to provide the basic services. NGOs could increase the provision of technical advice to the district line ministries along more development-oriented lines.

> **Development organizations and donors** should seriously consider integrated refugee programmes as a task on their agenda. The Self-Reliance Strategy provides an excellent starting point...to include refugees routinely as a target group in programmes for sector or regional development. This may require additional funding in order to cater for the additional target group.

> **The receiving country** will have to be supported and strengthened in their efforts to abandon obstacles and barriers to self-reliance, such as formal interdiction, for refugees to grow perennial crops....The new refugee bill ...should facilitate this process, but further implementing legislation will be needed. The Office of the Prime Minister should be assisted in convincing other line-ministries to provide the necessary assistance. It appears to be an important task for the Directorate for Refugees to advocate the Self-Reliance Strategy and to convince other government structures about expected positive effects.[15]

As stated by the government and UNCHR in their introduction to the Strategy paper, their hope was that "we will jointly succeed in our efforts to close the gap between "relief" and "development." Failure to cross traditional boundaries between these often-separated worlds would risk [leaving] the refugees and their host populations in a kind of developmental "no man's land" which in turn will lead to tension and conflict."

Some observers question the feasibility of integrating refugee assistance into the overall development program of the hosting district when refugees' own concerns are not adequately addressed. In particular, it is argued, in Uganda, that as refugee assistance is handed over to the host government as per SRS, refugees still do not enjoy freedom of movement and its associated socio-economic advantages. They also lack a political voice with which to participate in the decision-making processes that establish the conditions of how they live and work.[16] Self-reliance and other kinds of refugee integration programs should ensure that such initiatives address their legal status and rights, and are not only about facilitating socio-economic co-existence with host communities.

How has the SRS fared? According to Dryden-Petersen and Hovil in 2002, UNHCR Uganda said that while some refugees, such as those in Adjumani, "had become self-sufficient in terms of food production, [but] the upheavals of recent attacks and violence have caused refugees to flee their fields and become, once again dependent on direct assistance."[17] But no evaluation had been done, because—as Dryden-Petersen and Hovil report—UNHCR Uganda stated, "an evaluation in this context would not be productive."

As of 2003, the SRS was still being implemented by UNHCR, and it remains a funding priority for the UN in Uganda.[18] But, given the impact of continued security problems in the North, the humanitarian needs of internally displaced Ugandans have become greater than had originally been foreseen. Refugee numbers have remained high—reduced numbers of Sudanese refugees entering Uganda in 2002-3 were offset by an influx of close to 20,000 refugees from the DRC.

Security problems have derailed the SRS, but even without these, there were some problems with its conceptualization and implementation.[19] However, as a program in which the government and UNHCR worked together to support the livelihoods of refugees, while also trying to link relief and development, it set an important precedent. Other projects seeking to link refugee-relief with development have followed, in recent years. The Zambian Initiative is a collaborative project between UNHCR, the Zambian government, donors, and other UN agencies, which seeks to include Angolan refugees in a poverty-alleviation project in western Zambia. According to the Donor Report, the Zambian government "wishes to build on the positive aspect of the refugees, by including them in its attempt to alleviate poverty in the refugee hosting areas in the Western Province...and to create an improved and conducive situation for refugees to become productive members of their host communities." The Zambia Initiative is envisaged as "a model for donor coordination in poverty-reduction efforts, and a forum for harmonization of donor action in a situation that links relief and development."[20] Projects such as the ones in Uganda and Zambia—while still confronting many problems—offer models for future approaches that go beyond traditional relief.

NGOs: Supporting Refugee Livelihoods in Camps with Microfinance Services

One of the most serious livelihood obstacles for refugees is finding legitimate, non-exploitative sources of start-up credit. In recent years, some refugee agencies have experimented with providing microfinance services to economically-active refugees. Microfinance in developing countries, especially South Asia, has generated some success in poverty reduction, but it has not been widely attempted with refugees, because they are considered too risky an investment. However, as increasing numbers of refugees remain "stuck" in protracted situations, a number of NGOs have introduced microfinance services.

Microfinance services include microcredit (the provision of small loans, usually of less than one hundred dollars) and other financial services, such as savings or remittance facilities, that wouldn't otherwise be available to refugees. NGOs can provide savings opportunities for refugees, allowing them to keep their money in a separate account, or to move money back and forth between camps, and with their family and friends abroad who send them needed funds. Remittance services include providing access to formal money-transfer-institutions, including Western Union, or to informal ones, such as the Somalis' *hawilaad.*

Most commonly, NGOs provide microfinance services to refugees in the form of access to microcredit, in which small monetary loans are made to groups or to individuals, and repayment occurs in installments. Loans can bear interest, or a service charge can be imposed. The idea is that the livelihood enterprises of displaced people can be supported in ways that are in keeping with maintaining the borrowers' dignity as economic actors—not as recipients of charitable handouts.

Over the past ten years, microcredit practitioners have been developing standards for their programs, developing a common language and improving program quality. In-kind loan programs—such as seeds and tools, or livestock—are another form of livelihood support, intended for different purposes and used for various types of clients. Microcredit institutions are selective about where they start programs, and try not to implement them in settings where they will fail. The preconditions for a microcredit program include a reasonable degree of: security or stability; the reemergence of some market activity, and "a certain assurance that, when refugees or internally displaced persons are the focus, they will remain in place long enough for programs to make and recover loans (eighteen months is the common benchmark)."[21] These conditions can be found in many protracted refugee situations today, and they are also used in post-conflict countries to assist returning refugees. Where these conditions are in place, and where NGOs with some experience and expertise are implementing the program, microcredit programs can be successful for refugees. For example, American Refugee Committee (ARC) has working programs in Sierra Leone for returning-refugees and ex-combatants, and World Relief has successfully implemented microfinance programs in Rwanda and Mozambique.[22] Not all microfinance programs for refugees have been successful; and, a major reason they fail is due to bad practice on the part of NGOs or uncooperative governments. For example, in Cairo, the government refused to allow Save the Children to start a microcredit program for urban refugees,[23] because it did not want to extend any additional facilities to refugees. But several microcredit programs in refugee contexts have had very positive results, although their full impact on the livelihoods of refugees has yet to be fully assessed.

When microcredit programs are properly implemented, there is good evidence that they can work. Such programs require refugees to have solid business plans, and budgets that take into account the many market constraints they will face. Programs often provide training in business startup and development. Importantly, many relief organizations have realized that they should not become involved in microcredit if they do not have expertise in microcredit programs. Instead, in-kind loans should be used where monetary loans aren't appropriate, and it is imperative that they not be referred to as microcredit, because this will only muddy the water, confusing clients, donors, and practitioners. The following two case studies discuss two different types of credit programs found in camps: income-generation loans and microcredit.

CORD and Income Generation in the Kasulu Camps, Western Tanzania

One of UNHCR's implementing partners for Community Services is Christian Outreach for Relief and Development (CORD), which was formed in 1967, and is based in the UK. CORD operates in 11 countries in Africa, Eastern Europe, and Southeast and Central Asia, employing an expatriate staff of twenty-five, over six-hundred national staff members, and over 1,000 refugee.workers.[24] It has implemented agriculture, business, and community-building programs in relief and development settings for eleven years—in the Sudan, then in rural Cambodia, and other parts of Africa. In 1994, CORD responded to the Rwandan crisis by administering community service programs in two of the Kagera region refugee camps in Tanzania. Based on this experience, expatriate and national staff were re-deployed in 1997 to coordinate the Community Service program for UNHCR in the Kasulu camps—including Nyarugusu and Lugufu camps for Congolese refugees.

As CORD sees it, the primary purpose of Community Services is to enable communities and individuals to have greater control over their lives, and to mobilize and encourage the community to support their most vulnerable members. Support is given through income generating initiatives, and the skills base of the population is enhanced through education, vocational skills training, literacy and awareness raising.

The camps were set up in 1997, in response to the influx of Congolese refugees, mainly from the Uvira area of South Kivu. Both camps are located in the Kasulu region of western Tanzania near the border with Burundi and near Lake Tanganyika. Nyarugusu camp is located some 80 km north of the town of Kasulu, and Lugufu Camp is 75 km south of Kasulu. In this protracted situation, Congolese refugees must deal with increasing government restrictions on their freedom of movement and other economic rights, as well as reduced humanitarian aid, and declining interest by the donor community. Limited access to land coupled with poor soil conditions make it difficult for refugees to grow enough food to sustain themselves. Recently the Tanzanian government terminated the right of refugees to leave the camp, even with a permit, without the supervision of Tanzanian staff. Limited access to the surrounding area has greatly limited the cash economy within the camp. In addition, between February and July 2003, maize rations were cut to 50% by the World Food Program (WFP), and now people are unable to sell off surplus maize or trade it for other commodities. This limits opportunities for trade and commerce. Refugees do not have the right to work, and few have capital to start livelihoods. Some refugees are resorting to harmful or risky strategies in order to sustain their livelihoods. Most of the refugees, in both camps, however, have become adept at using the limited resources available. Many have begun small businesses, and trade with local people occurs in the camp market. Informal credit practices in the camp are based on moneylenders and rotating savings and credit groups. Moneylenders are part of a credit system known as *Banque Lambert*, in which an individual or a group of individuals lends to clients and charges interest of between 18% to 30% (even as high as 50%) of the loan. A survey conducted by CORD revealed that 62% of those interviewed thought *Banque Lambert* was useful but that lenders could be intimidating and threatening. The rotating credit system known as *Likilimba*, familiar to those from the DRC, is practiced in the camps. The *Likilimba* system (or "likelemba" as it is known in Kinshasa) is a rotating system of borrowing money within a group. Each member contributes a fixed amount every month and gets the whole lot by turns. However, the cash flow in the camp is insufficient to maintain an economy of small businesses in a way that encourages people to join up and develop businesses for profit.

CORD's livelihood initiatives are based on existing group structures and traditional credit systems that are familiar to refugees. Accordingly, CORD supports rotating forms of credit, both of livestock and of cash. The revolving livestock scheme is based on ducks, which are hardy in a camp environment. Each group member is provided with breeding pairs of ducks and the offspring is passed to the next group member, and so on. (An attempted chicken project was less successful as chickens are more susceptible to diseases than are ducks.) CORD began a rotating credit program based on the *Liklimba* system at the end of 2002, after several meetings with community groups highlighted the need for credit. Existing groups of five were identified in each zone in the camp. The groups had to have been already established before the program started, to ensure that the groups were not just formed in response to the program. Each group received a small loan (about $60), repayable over 6 months, at an interest rate of 2%. After the first groups completed their repayment cycle, additional groups received loans after an orientation and training in basic book keeping and marketing.

As a way to ensure that the refugee community "owned" the program, each of the seven zones in the camp formed a voluntary credit committee of five people including the zone leader. The loan committees were tasked to supervise and monitor daily progress of the loans. The committee members received training in credit concepts, book-keeping, marketing and in basic conflict resolution techniques. The committees jointly drew up their own terms of reference and conditions of service, which include the following:

- Receiving loan requests, assessing and make loan recommendations;
- Taking part in resolving group misunderstandings;
- Advising groups on their business progress and credit repayment;
- Conducting follow up with groups and encouraging repayment;
- Intervening with defaulter groups and reporting this to CORD;
- Preparing a bi-weekly zonal credit progress report and submit to CORD.

CORD has sought to give the refugees control over their affairs, including in the management of income generating programs. While problems can emerge, and such programs are not perfect, they offer ways of envisioning a different approach to that of traditional relief handouts.

American Refugee Committee and Microcredit Programs in Guinea

American Refugee Committee (ARC) was a pioneer in the use of microcredit with refugees and displaced persons. It started its first microcredit program in Guinea in 1997, serving refugees from Sierra Leone and Liberia, especially women. ARC has created a model that includes training in health and literacy, and on-going business support for its clients. The program seeks to increase self-sufficiency and reduce dependence on food-aid. One goal is to enable those with risky livelihoods, like prostitution, to make a livelihood change.

ARC started its first microcredit program in the Nzerekore camps in Guinea in 1997, serving refugees from Sierra Leone and Liberia. ARC was a pioneer in the use of microcredit with refugees and internally displaced persons, and has developed a model program that includes training in health and literacy, and on-going business support for its clients. ARC's microcredit program is a step-up one, in which vulnerable clients or new arrivals form groups and begin with a start-up grant, than progress to a basic loan and then to an advanced loan. The three-step micro-credit program begins with a *starter grant* of $50 provided to groups of 2-3 women to initiate small enterprises. Repayment must occur in three months, with no interest. In step two, after repayment of the starter grant, groups of 5-7 people, mostly women, can apply for a *basic loan* of $65 per person in the group to repay in 6 months with no interest. The third step is the *advanced loan* of $100 per client, given to self-formed groups of 3-4 people to repay in 4-6 months with 5% interest. From January–August 2003, the first cycle of start-up grants totaling about $11.000 were distributed in Laine refugee camp to 483 women, divided into 231 groups. Of these, 210 were eligible for the second cycle—the basic loan. The other groups did not qualify for the second cycle because one of their members did not pass the eligibility criteria, i.e. retain at least 70% of the original grant in the business and reinvest 50% of the profits/gains. In 2004, the emphasis shifted to the disbursement of advanced loans for clients who had successfully reimbursed their basic loans.

All start-up grant and loan clients receive business training classes. In addition business classes were given to students of their vocational training schools and to primary and secondary school teachers and female teaching assistants. ARC estimates that in 2003 over 500 individuals "non-ARC/IGP" clients have been trained. According to ARC's records, 93 percent of their clients' were still in business two years after the initial loan was issued, and the program's repayment rates are at 96 percent.[25] In addition, once repatriation to Sierra Leone began in 2001, ARC has begun a "Refugees to Return" program, which links the microcredit program in the camp with one in Sierra Leone. The *Refuge to Return* approach links financial services to refugees in their country of refuge with those in their country of return through a transferable credit history methodology. By applying sound microfinance practices and providing the necessary incentives for repayment, ARC has successfully provided loans to Sierra Leonean refugees in Guinea and Liberia, and built a leading microfinance institution in Sierra Leone to serve them upon their return. While offering general lessons for service provision to mobile populations, this approach also provides a refugee/IDP assistance model for promoting self-reliance and sustainable repatriation and reintegration.

Challenges

One of the challenges for camp-based microfinance programs is that they must operate alongside traditional relief programs, i.e. where UNHCR and other NGOs hand out "free" relief, or in the form of non-repayable grants. Large numbers of refugees in the camp, are too poor or "vulnerable" to be helped with microfinance and need this traditional relief, but its presence in the camp undermines the idea that more able-bodied people can receive loans which must be repaid. Since many credit programs are based on revolving loans, repayment is necessary for the next in line to receive a loan. But if refugees see a loan as part of the UNHCR-distributed relief to which they are entitled, they will resist paying it back. For this reason, microfinance organizations in camps try to distance themselves from UNHCR and other relief-based agencies as much as possible. This is not always possible, especially for those who are implementing partners of UNHCR.

Beyond International Assistance: Local Organizations

The official and most publicized form of refugee assistance is the system constituted by UNHCR and its network of implementing and operational partners. However, there are a variety of local and community-based organizations and initiatives that also seek to enable refugees to pursue livelihoods. Many of these operate in contexts of protracted conflict where self-settled refugees and internally displaced people live together with nondisplaced people also affected by conflict. Such regions include, for example, the conflict-ravaged zones on either side of the Sudan-Uganda border, the Kivus region of eastern Congo, the Kenya-Somalia border region, Liberia, the Iran-Afghanistan border zone, and the Burmese-Thai border zone.

In these conflict-affected regions, UNHCR's presence is relatively small, since there are few camps, and in general international humanitarian assistance is hard to come by. While there are some UN organizations present,[26] such as OCHA or UNICEF, most of the livelihoods initiatives are undertaken by local community-based organizations formed in response to the needs of their community. Because refugees and IDPs are part of the community, they are included. Funding support is erratic, and comes from a range of possible sources, including different UN agencies, donors like the EU and USAID, and private sources. Some examples of these kinds of programs are discussed below.

A Boat Project: Terekaka, Southern Sudan

The village of Terekaka is a two-four hour boat journey down the Nile from the town of Juba, in northern Bahr el Jabl State, which until 2004, was one of the worst affected states in the war zone of southern Sudan. Control of Bahr el Jabl was heavily contested and during June-August 2002, two of the state's six administrative units, including Terekaka's, were controlled by the Sudan Peoples Liberation Army (SPLA). The region is populated mainly by agro-pastoralists like the Mundari, who traditionally rely on cattle for income, food security and social stability. Conflict and displacement led to the loss of many livestock, and Terekaka experienced an influx of internally displaced pastoralists, as well as Congolese refugees fleeing the war in eastern Congo.

The village of Terekaka illustrates the loss and gain of different kinds of capital as a result of conflict and displacement. Physical capital—cattle—were lost to raiding or because the pastoralists had to flee fighting and leave their cattle behind. Conflict has reduced access to natural capital—traditional pastureland. On the other hand, the Congolese refugees who moved into Terekaka brought with them human capital in the form of boat building and fishing skills. Both the displaced and their hosts have had to diversify their livelihoods. One alternative source of income is the plentiful fish in the surrounding lakes and rivers. Although the Mundari have traditionally had a disdain for fish—both as a food, and for anyone who worked with fish—the realization that fish is an important commodity changed this attitude. During the year 2000, approximately seven tons of fish were harvested and transported to Juba for sale in the markets there.

A Sudanese community-based organization, Accomplish, which is based in Juba and works in Terekaka, learned that one constraint in the marketing of the fish is the cost and difficulty of transporting the fish from Terekeka to Juba. This expense takes up most of the profit from selling the fish. Accomplish discussed options with the community and it was agreed that a boat was needed. In August 2002, a fiberglass boat with an outboard motor was purchased through a grant from a small foundation.[27] The boat was intended to serve the community's transportation needs including taking goods—mainly fish, but also ducks, charcoal, and ground nuts produced by a women's Self-Help Group—and people between Terekaka and Juba.

A Goat Project in Masisi region, North Kivu, Eastern DRC

The livelihood context for the people of the eastern Congo is one of on-going conflict, insecurity, and recurring displacement. In the town of Goma, a local consortium of 40 farmers and veterinarians known as CREDAP (Committee for Reflection on Agro-Pastoral Development) was founded in the early 1990s, with the aim of helping to rebuild the livelihoods of the agriculturalists and pastoralists in North Kivu in ways that would both support conflict-affected communities and encourage a reduction in tensions leading to conflict. CREDAP identifies potential livestock programs, and makes recommendations to donors seeking to support economic development in conflict zones. CREDAP has identified 29 sites in North Kivu where they implement and monitor programs.

One of CREDAP's goat rotation programs takes place in the province of Masisi, a fertile, hilly region of North Kivu, some 70 km north-west of Goma. Prior to the violent conflict of the 1990s which has devastated the eastern Congo, this was a productive coffee growing and cattle ranching area. Cheese-making and abattoirs were common commercial activities. Since the war, the cattle have been looted or killed and there is no commercial coffee production, or any other (legal) commercial activity, except for some areas where cattle are being reintroduced by warlords. The villages dotting the hills eke out a living with subsistence agriculture and a few goats. Chronic fear of raiding militias inhibits economic activity, and most villages host high proportions of displaced people.

CREDAP's project focused on three neighboring villages, Nyamitaba, Kichanga and Buranga. Goats were purchased to be used as the rotating fund for each village. In goat rotation programs, participants receive one female breeding goat and must pay back the first baby goat after it is weaned from its mother. The rotation occurs approximately every 6-8 months, when the next set of goats is given to the selected villagers next in the queue. About half of all female goats give birth to twins, so the number of goats in a village can grow rapidly. In Masisi, meat goats are raised for their resale value and not used for milk. A goat credit program is believed to be a less risky investment in a conflict-zone because goats are more easily moved (if their owners must hide them or flee), less susceptible to illness, and more adaptable than other forms of livestock, such as cattle. Goats are also less expensive than cattle (a female goat costs approximately $50 versus a cow which can start at $200), and more can be purchased with the available budget, thereby increasing the number of villagers who benefit.

Rotating livestock is an indigenous form of community credit, well known and understood by villagers, and widespread in many rural areas of Africa. It is the kind of livelihood intervention that is easily supported by external funders, and given the relatively low cost outlay, has a high impact on displaced people's ability to restart their livelihoods and derive both personal and household benefits. In Masisi, the women reported that extra income from the goats contributed to household food security (by improving the variety and amount of food), and helped pay for transportation, and health and school fees. The women also said that owning goats gave them a sense of self-worth. These kinds of programs can also have indirect positive outcomes. In Terekaka, the boat also served to provide transport at reduced costs to veterinarians and health workers, which facilitated vaccination and immunization campaigns for riverine communities and their cattle along the White Nile.

Tension and Security Problems

In conflict-affected communities, providing scarce resources like capital equipment (boats) or livestock (goats) can have potential negative consequences, and it is important that these risks be monitored. The arrival of new livelihood assets can create tensions, and possibly render the recipients more vulnerable than they were before. For example, in Terekaka, the boat's arrival increased competition in the marketing of fish and new fishing cooperatives formed—along with increased tensions in the community. The appearance of a significant economic resource in the form of the boat can create strong community reactions, as various individuals try to gain control of the resource. These kinds of issues and problems can be managed in different ways, such as by creating a central management committee, but it is important that tensions be monitored and the community stay involved in resolving them.

The appearance of new resources can also make communities vulnerable to predators. In Terekaka, the boat was commandeered by SPLA forces on one occasion, and passage on the river is frequently threatened by the presence of Lords Resistance Army rebels from Uganda in the region. Thus, while the boat facilitates livelihoods, it also exposes people to security risks. Similarly, in North Kivu, new goats in the villages could make the villages targets for raids by rebel forces.

For organizations selecting program sites and clients, there is always the concern that this selection will be perceived to have an ethnic dimension. When resources are selectively provided to people in conflict-affected regions, there is a risk of being perceived as corrupt or biased, especially if program officers are from a local ethnic group, or if they are themselves refugees. The problem of perceived favoritism and unfairness can arise both within a community and across the wider region. A concern about the Masisi goat credit program was that once word got out that the villages received goats, they could become the target of envy by neighboring villages, leading to new tensions and even violence.

How to address these concerns? One approach is to leave the decision about whether to take the risk in accepting new resources up to the community involved, who are most aware of potential security problems and can best assess risk. This assumes that community discussions would encompass all members, and not just those who would benefit most. Another safeguard is to ensure that the criteria for participant selection be transparent, and that these criteria are perceived to be fair by everyone in the community. When the decision is made to target specific groups in the community, such as war widows or demobilized combatants, the reasons for this decision should be aired and discussed in the community. Charges of unfairness and favoritism should also be aired in public fora. In general, programs do better when information about decisions and program management is actively disseminated, and the participation of the broader community is solicited. In the Masisi villages, CREDAP members regularly visit the villages and meet with the community leaders and the community to explain (again) the program, how beneficiaries are selected, and to hear the community voice problems and grievances.

In some cases, the community itself has ideas about how credit programs can be used to reduce tensions. In Masisi, one village committee came up with the idea that in order to reduce ethnic tension within the community, the rotation would occur across ethnic lines, so that a recipient would pay back her baby goat to a woman of a different ethnic group who was next in line. These are admittedly small impacts, and difficult to measure, but they need to be seen in the larger picture of small actions among many affected communities that can contribute to a gradual lessening of tension and conflict.

Conclusions and Persistent Challenges

The idea that all refugees, no matter how capable they are of supporting themselves, are entitled to and should receive "free" relief is well-established in the minds of both traditional refugee agencies and many refugees. In an age of shrinking assistance, this mindset will have to change, and so will the existing model of camps maintained through ever decreasing levels so food aid and other relief services. Supporting the ability of displaced people to pursue livelihoods is an important way of going beyond traditional relief assistance, both from a humanitarian point of view, and from a human security perspective. Livelihoods assistance will have to come from sources other than official humanitarian aid. These alternate sources include the funds provided by small, private foundations, which in aggregate can often amount to substantial amounts, especially in the context of aid-deprived conflict regions. Small grants have the advantage of flexibility and strategic targeting, and a shorter bureaucratic time line. One problem with such funding sources, however, is that it is necessary to identify local organizations or community representatives, who will administer the funds in cooperation with the foundation. Finding the appropriate local partner to do this is a significant challenge.[28]

In conflict- and displaced-affected communities, cash and credit are one of the primary needs for economic survival. How people gain access to financial resources depends on their communities and networks, as well as humanitarian assistance. New approaches and modalities are needed to rejuvenate livelihood programs, and experiments must be attempted. However, in trying new approaches, it is crucial that humanitarian agencies don't add to the vulnerability of people in conflict zones. One way is to draw on the experience and local knowledge of established communities. This means that programs must address everyone in the community, both host and displaced. It is a mistake to target displaced people while excluding the host communities in which they live and which often support them. In many cases, the host community is as badly off as the displaced people living among them. Providing only the displaced with aid or livelihood resources is unfair, unethical, unsustainable and ineffective. Helping both hosts and displaced is sound policy for the displaced too—they are more likely to be welcomed and assisted by the community when everyone benefits from humanitarian assistance.

Another caveat concerns the import of new policy initiatives seeking to support displaced livelihoods. Initiatives like microcredit, that had success in one region, such as Bangladesh, may be destined for failure in other regions like Sub Saharan Africa, if differences in formal and informal institutional arrangements are not taken into account. Similarly, initiatives that work in more stable development settings, could fail in unstable settings of displacement.[29]

What can international NGOs do to influence the national (host country) policy environment in which they work? Working either at the grass roots level (with refugees or the local population) or at the international level (with donors and international organizations) is sometimes easier than working with governments and their bureaucracies, especially those branches that are in remote outposts where refugees are found. Advocating for policy changes that support refugee livelihoods requires taking on difficult country-wide problems. For example, when governments won't allow refugees to access arable land or move freely outside of camps or work, it is often because arable land is already contested by nationals, and because unemployment is high in host countries.

In zones of conflict and displacement, livelihood support programs work well when they are small-scale, strategically positioned and flexible, so as to be able to quickly take advantage of windows of opportunity. The only way to do this is to build relationships with local partners based on trust, and which solicit real input and advice from the community. Many traditional income generating and microfinance programs fail because they are based on inadequate understanding of and adaptation to the local context. A top-down, headquarters-driven approach is used which doesn't take into account the security, politics and economics of the local setting. Livelihood support programs for refugees should be locally appropriate, that is, customized for the community and with the local market in mind. To do this, donors must identify and work with local partners—NGOs usually—who have deep and longstanding knowledge about the region. This will usually mean that the local partner has key contacts with the major political and military players in the region, including rebel leaders and warlords.

In turn, this will mean that the local partner is not trusted or regarded as neutral by everyone in the community. While it is rarely the case that everyone in the community trusts a particular local NGO, *most* of the community should not view it as corrupt, inefficient, on the take or under some faction's sway.

Notes

1   See Crisp, "No Solutions."

2   Shelly Dick, "Review of CORD Community Services for Congolese Refugees in Tanzania" EPAU/2002/13 (December 2002): 4; available at www .unhcr.ch/cgi-bin/texis/vtx/home?page=search.

3   For in-depth discussion and case studies of "warehousing," see USCRI, "World Refugee Survey, 2004."

4   Personal communication with the author.

5   See for example, Anderson, *Do No Harm.*

6   Arafat Jamal, *Minimum Standards and Essential Needs in a Protracted Refugee Situation. A Review of the UNHCR Programme in Kakuma, Kenya,* report for UNHCR Evaluation and Policy Unit EPAU/2000/05, November 2000, 28; Tania Kaiser, "UNHCR's Withdrawal from Kiryandongo: Anatomy of a Handover," (working paper, New Issues in Refugee Research, no. 32, UNHCR, 2000), 6.

7   See Jamal, *Minimum Standards* for a discussion of UNHCR's approach to the local Turkana population round Kakuma camp in Kenya.

8   Kaiser, "UNHCR's Withdrawal," 6.

9   *The Community Services Function in UNHCR: An Independent Evaluation,* report for UNHCR Evaluation and Policy Unit EPAU/2003/02, March 2003, 118. The evolution of Community Services in UNHCR is described as follows: in 1989, UNHCR was looking for a field approach that focused on the productive capacities of refugees themselves and encouraged self-reliance, participatory development, and cost-saving mechanisms. Reflecting a renewed interest in "community development," it sought to harness the "community's"capacities and reduce dependency through a more concerted "developmental approach." As part of this shift in strategy, Social Services was renamed Community Services. The name change also served to reinforce the idea of the community as a participant in finding solutions, particularly in the context of protracted refugee situations.

10   See "UNHCR, Refugee Livelihoods and Self-Reliance: A Brief History" under *Research/Evaluation* at www.unhcr.ch.

11   Protracted situations are seen as having negative consequences for host states, local populations and for national and regional security. Refugees trapped in camps for years on end, without any hope for the future, are much more likely to become involved in military and criminal activities.

12   See "UNHCR, Refugee Livelihoods."

13   For more about Guinea see Barbara Reeds, *Assessing Refugee Self-Reliance: A Food Economy Assessment. Kountaya and Telikoro Refugee Camps, Kissidougou, Guinea*, UNHCR Evaluation and Policy Unit Background Document, October 31, 2002; for Ghana see Dick, "Liberians in Ghana."

14   See Dryden-Peterson and Hovil, "Local Integration"; Macchiavello, "Forced Migrants"; Wiebke Hoeing, "Self-Image and the Well-Being of Refugees in Rhino Camp, Uganda," (working paper, New Issues in Refugee Research, no. 103, UNHCR, 2004).

15   Government of Uganda and UNHCR, *Self Reliance Strategy (1999-2003) for Refugee Hosting Areas in Moyo, Aruna and Adjumani Districts, Uganda*, Report of the Midterm Review: RLSS Mission Report, April 2004; available at www.unhcr.ch/

16   See Tania Kaiser's objections raised in "Participation, Self-Reliance and Integration: Sudanese Refugees in Uganda," *IDI Insights 44* (December 2002); available at www.id21.org/insights/insights44/insights-iss 44-art04.html.

17   Dryden-Peterson and Hovil, "Local Integration," 11.

18   According to the 2003 UN Mid-Year Review for Uganda, "In line with the [SRS],…several activities are being carried out in Arua, Adjumani and Moyo districts in partnership with NGOs and the relevant district offices. Activities are being selected corresponding to implementation capacity and the priorities identified by the district offices for the integration of refugees service into the district programme. The levels of integration vary from district to district. Together with the GoU, appropriate action will be taken by UNHCR to refine the SRS further in the Northern districts, to expand it to other refugee-impacted districts, and to involve other actors in the process. Activities planned for the second half of 2003 include the revival of National SRS Task Force (comprised of GoU, UNHCR and several NGOs), the continued sensitization of district authorities and an evaluation of the SRS." See www.reliefweb.int.

19   Dryden-Peterson and Hovil, "Local integration," 7.

20   For more see Government of Zambia and UNHCR, *Zambia Initiative: Refugee-Hosting Community Development Programme*, Donors Mission Report (March 18-28, 2002) and Government of Zambia and UNHCR,

The Zambia Initiative: In Pursuit of Sustainable Solutions for Refugees in Zambia, May 1, 2004. Both these reports are available on UNHCR's Web site at www.unhcr.ch.

21 Karen Doyle, "Microfinance in the Wake of Conflict: Challenges and Opportunities," The SEEP Network, (1998); available at www.usaid.gov/ our_work/crosscutting_programs/conflict/publications/other_usaid.html.

22 See *Alchemy Project Annual Report 2004*, Alchemy Project (Feinstein International Famine Center, Tufts University, Medford, MA, 2002); available at famine.tufts.edu/index.html?id=18.

23 Sperl, *Evaluation.*

24 Information is taken from CORD, *Self Reliance in Nyarugusu and Lugufu Camp with Congolese Refugees, Kasulu District, Western Tanzania*, internal report (Lemington Spa, UK: CORD, 2003).

25 *Alchemy Project Annual Report 2004.*

26 The United Nations Relief and Works Agency for Palestine Refugees (UNRWA)'s Microfinance and Microenterprise Programme (MMP) in the West Bank and Gaza Strip was launched in June 1991 following the outbreak of the first *intifadah* in1987 and the Gulf War. It provides working capital loans to Palestinians, in an effort to reduce poverty and economically empower refugees. Since the project began over 50,000 loans have been made. See UNWRA Web site: www.un.org/unrwa/programmes/mmp/ overview.html.

27 See *Alchemy Project Annual Report 2004.*

28 Tania Kaiser "Participatory and Beneficiary-Based Approaches to the Evaluation of Humanitarian Programmes," (working paper, New Issues in Refugee Research, no. 51, UNHCR, 2002).

29 For more on the lessons learned from implementing microcredit in refugee situations see Jeff Flowers, "Microfinance and Internally Displaced Persons in Azerbaijan," paper for UNHCR Refugees Livelihood Network, FINCA Azerbaijan (November 21, 2003); Timothy H. Nourse, "Microfinance for Refugees Emerging Principles for Effective Implementation," paper for UNHCR Refugees Livelihood Network, ARC (2003) (Both papers available under *Research/Evaluation* at www.unhcr.ch); and Jacobsen and Bailey. "Micro-Credit," 99-102.

Chapter 6

Supporting the Livelihoods of Refugees: A Model for Refugee Assistance

T he world's 12 million or so refugees constitute a relatively small proportion of the tens of millions of displaced people living in countries devastated by poverty and violent conflict. Compared with those who are internally displaced, most refugees are better off: they have escaped the invisibility and lack of protection faced by those trapped in their home countries. A stark example currently in the news is the millions of people who have been forced from their homes in Sudan's western Darfur region by the violence committed by marauding militias supported by the Khartoum government. Those who have managed to cross the border into Chad have been able to access some humanitarian assistance. But those who are stuck in Sudan have little assistance or protection beyond that allowed by the Khartoum government. Unlike internally displaced people, refugees are the responsibility of the international community embodied by the UNHCR, which works together with the host government to ensure the safety of refugees.

The system of refugee assistance and protection that has evolved since 1950 now exhibits serious flaws and is in need of significant rethinking. The problem is that the current system is dominated by the emergency phase. Humanitarian assistance is set up to address the physical needs of refugees when they first flee across the border, and, to a large extent, these needs are met by UNHCR and its NGO implementing partners. It is the period that follows the emergency—the so-called "care and maintenance" phase—that needs reworking. This phase continues to be shaped by the belief that refugees are temporary guests who will soon repatriate—a solution desired by aid agencies, the host community, and most refugees themselves. However, millions of refugees remain stuck in the limbo between the emergency phase and repatriation (or resettlement for a lucky few). In this care and maintenance phase, as media interest fades and refugees become invisible to the public eye, the humanitarian budget shrinks and assistance levels decline. Restrictive measures, such as the deportation of asylum-seekers, are often introduced by governments to limit what is seen as "irregular migration" and the misuse of the asylum system. Host governments not only require refugees to live in remote and insecure camps, but also impose all kinds of obstacles to refugees' ability to engage in economic activities or otherwise find work. These restrictive measures are unlikely to be dismantled soon.[1]

Refugee-populated areas are often among the least developed and most remote border areas of host countries, far from the logistical reach or political interest of the capital. In many host countries, humanitarian services for refugees exist in parallel to a separate but often underfunded set of services for the surrounding population. Refugees and nationals live apart, with separate systems for food and nutrition, education, health, and water and sanitation. As in all cases where such separation exists, the systems are far from equal, and often the balance tilts in favor of the refugees when it comes to meeting basic needs. Although relief agencies and UNHCR pay lip service to avoiding the creation of parallel systems, at best this is represented by granting locals access to refugee health services or by providing funds for refugees to attend local secondary schools. On the other hand, when it comes to economic activities like trade or employment or working the land, it is the refugees who are at the disadvantage. Parallel and unequal systems represent an enormous waste of resources and an unfair and politically indefensible distribution of resources. This situation is recognized by the humanitarian community, but until recently, little has been done about it.

Given this situation of prolonged displacement coupled with both reluctance by governments to host refugees and inequitable systems of parallel services, what is the best and most realistic way to assist and protect refugees? Is there a way in which international refugee assistance can be designed to include host populations, who are often as poorly off as the refugees and who face their own economic and security problems?

This closing chapter attempts to sketch out a refugee policy—based on a livelihoods and local development approach—that could potentially improve the lot of both refugees and host populations in protracted situations. The model refugee policy is based on three guiding principles: provision of a designated zone of residence, accordance of rights and obligations in the host countries, and provision of services through the local community. Taking into account the current political climate of growing restrictions on refugees, the model calls for certain restrictions on refugees and asylum-seekers, as well as rights for them. The feasibility of the model is discussed in the light of current refugee policies in countries like Zambia, Mozambique, and Sierra Leone, which approximate the model. The proposed model is intended to offer a challenge and to stimulate debate on how to shape refugee assistance in ways that support displaced livelihoods.

A Proposed Model for Refugee Assistance in Protracted Situations

There are many reasons to abolish refugee camps and parallel systems of aid as they operate today, but there must be a viable alternative. Such an alternative must incorporate the political realities in host countries without pandering to them, and it must go beyond the traditional relief model so as to shift refugee policy in a direction that is sustainable both from a humanitarian perspective and in terms of the host country's national interests. This section sets out some of the underlying assumptions and guiding principles of such a policy in countries of first asylum. The model is not fully articulated; it is hoped that further discussion and debate will identify its flaws and promote its strengths.

First, let us make the following assumptions about asylum-seekers and refugees in countries of first asylum (host countries):

1. Host governments make distinctions between different groups of asylum-seekers according to such categories as nationality and ethnicity, and differentiate in the treatment of them. For example, a host government might grant full refugee status to some groups (who become Convention refugees) and not to others (who remain *prima facie* refugees or asylum-seekers).

2. Those who are granted formal (Convention) refugee status are the minority in host countries, outnumbered by asylum-seekers, many of whom will never get formal refugee status.

3. Host governments are becoming increasingly restrictive toward refugees and asylum-seekers and are unlikely to permit all asylum-seekers to move, live, and work freely in the host country. Host governments are increasingly likely to restrict asylum-seekers to designated zones and camps.

4. In protracted refugee situations, levels of international humanitarian assistance will decline over time, both in terms of quality and quantity.

Given these assumptions, a refugee policy based on the three principles is set out below. It is important to note that the model is intended to represent the *minimum requirements* for a host country—any policy that goes beyond these principles and provides more rights and freedoms for refugees and asylum-seekers is to be applauded and supported.

The model is intended for asylum-seekers or *prima facie* refugees who have not been granted Convention status. Once an asylum seeker has obtained formal refugee status, he or she should be allowed to live among the host population and enter the immigration channels of the host country *en route* to permanent residence, if desired.

Principles for a Refugee Policy in Countries of First Asylum

1. *Place of residence.* Host countries should designate a zone of legal residence for asylum-seekers, which should be a secure and dignified place for all those living or working there and one that is targeted for refugee assistance. In host countries bordering sending countries, such a designated area or zone should be near the

border but at a safe distance from the conflict, and the area should be within range of a town. The designated area could include secure camps or settlements for refugees, but refugees also should be allowed to settle among the local population. While asylum-seekers should be required to *reside* in these areas, they should not be *restricted* to them, as the next principle explains.

2. *Rights and obligations in host countries.* All asylum-seekers should be accorded the economic and social rights assigned to them in the relevant international charters and laws, particularly the 1951 Convention and Protocol. These include, in particular:

    • *Freedom of movement and the right to work.* While residents in designated zones, asylum-seekers should be permitted to move about freely, including outside the zones, to engage in legal economic activities such as paid employment, private enterprise, and so forth.
    • *Documentation.* Asylum-seekers (and refugees) should be provided with documentation in the form of a refugee identity card that states their legal presence and address in the country and gives permission to travel within and outside the country.
    • *The right to remain.* Asylum-seekers who have lived in the host country under legal circumstances for an agreed-upon length of time (for instance, more than five years) should be eligible for permanent residence in accordance with the immigration laws of the host country as they pertain to long-term legal residents. Naturalization or citizenship is not necessary, however, if a host government is willing to grant it, this is a step to be applauded.
    • *Living within the law.* Refugees and asylum-seekers are under the obligation to abide by the civil and criminal laws of the host country, as well as regulations imposed by local authorities in host areas. Refugees who engage in criminal activity or actions undermining the security of the host country, should be deprived of their refugee or asylum seeker rights, and be treated according to the laws of the country.

3. *Provision of services.* There should be no parallel system. In designated zones, education, health, and financial services needed by both refugees and nonrefugees, should be provided through the local community, and refugees should have full access to them. This will require that international refugee assistance boost existing community services to offset any burden imposed by the refugees. Specialized services that address the needs of the forcibly displaced, such as emergency health and nutrition services, trauma

counseling, family tracing, and legal aid, should be provided separately to those who need them.

This model differs from most advocacy positions in that it does not call for full integration of asylum-seekers (or *prima facie* refugees), but rather envisions them as guests who are to be treated with dignity and respect and assisted with the problems associated with violence-induced flight, but not permitted the full range of rights assigned to citizens or to refugees with formal status. A model that advocates residence restrictions is bound to be criticized, and indeed there are potential risks, including the possibility that designated areas could become ghettos or marginalized places—as many camps are today. We will return to this and other concerns as the model is further discussed using illustrative case material from host countries where aspects of the model are or have been in place.

Principle I: Designated Zones of Residence

Rather than allowing asylum-seekers to live anywhere in the country, a designated zone of residence for refugees is advocated for two sets of reasons: the interests of asylum-seekers and those who work with them, and the need to acknowledge the political realities in host countries today.

Asylum-seekers' interests are better served when they reside in a designated zone, where they are assigned full economic rights, for the following reasons:

- Their security can be better monitored than if they are dispersed throughout the country—and lost to watchful international eyes;
- Those with special needs can be identified and assisted by international aid agencies;
- Government personnel (police, immigration officials, local authorities) and the private sector (employers, banks) in the zone will be familiar with the appropriate documentation, and asylum-seekers will not be at risk of employers or police not recognizing or understanding their rights to work and move around freely;
- The burden of the asylum-seekers' presence on the local population can be offset by aid resources that are targeted at social and economic infrastructure in the zone.

One of the advantages of a designated zone is that "protection by presence" is more possible because aid agencies and UN organizations can target their efforts and keep a watchful eye on the security of asylum-seekers. While asylum-seekers can and do survive out of the purview of aid agencies, they are not well served in such circumstances. This is illustrated by the problems faced by urban refugees, mostly asylum-seekers, who struggle without assistance and where local authorities like the police often fail to recognize their refugee identity cards. Such refugees are constantly at risk of having their goods confiscated or being arrested or deported. While some urban refugees are able to survive without assistance and can cope with official inter-ference, many others have made their way to urban areas only because there is no possibility of surviving economically in remote camps. Without assistance, their plight is often much worse than that of other urban poor.

A second set of reasons why designated zones should be incorporated into refugee policy concerns the political context of host counties as it relates to refugees and immigration in general. Their legal control over their territory gives govern-ments the right to determine where refugees should live, and Article 9 of the 1951 Convention gives governments some leeway "in time of war or other grave and exceptional circumstances" to decide how persons who have not yet been deter-mined to be refugees—that is, asylum-seekers—should be treated.[2] Since many gov-ernments consider conflicts on their borders to be threats to national security, they increasingly require refugees to live in camps and impose restrictions on their activ-ities. Given these threats as well as the domestic politics and local antagonism towards refugees in many countries of first asylum, it will be difficult to persuade governments to move in a more liberal direction that allows asylum-seekers to live anywhere they please. South Africa, one of the few countries in Africa that does not currently have an encampment policy, appears to be changing course and is rumored to be in the process of setting up camps along its northern border with Zimbabwe. A model of refugee policy must take these political realities into account without allowing them to dictate fully how refugees will be treated. We must find ways to work within the political context of the host country while still seeking the best options for refugees.

Designated zones allow host governments more control over asylum-seekers, at least in theory, and this makes it more likely that governments will allow asylum-seekers to live outside camps. However, refugee camps will persist, either by gov-ernment decree or sometimes because refugees themselves prefer to live in them. Camps are not necessarily destructive and disempowering places; refugees living in camps often score better on health, education, and other empowerment measures than do the local people and the self-settled refugees living outside the camp.[3] As a base in which to recover from the ordeal of flight and from which to go about put-ting one's life back together, a refugee camp need be no worse a place—and is pos-sibly a better one—than the surrounding community. Needed relief services can be provided, and camps can be places to rest and recover. As long as these areas are not allowed to sink into destitution and marginalization as refugee situations become protracted, they can increase refugees' well-being and access to resources and rights. On what does this depend? The ingredients for ensuring that camps or designated zones are places of security and dignity are set out in the next section.

Principle II: Rights and Obligations in Host Countries

For designated zones, including camps, to be humane and safe places of residence for asylum-seekers, aid agencies, donors, the host government, the local community, and the refugees themselves must work together to ensure several key elements.

The primary requirement is security. Governments should be encouraged and supported to train and equip their police and military forces so that they are familiar with refugee rights and with the kinds of security problems refugees face. These security problems include the presence of combatants living among refugees (according to international refugee law, only civilians can reside in camps), high rates of crime and domestic violence, impunity from criminal offences, and threats and harassment by the host community. This is not necessarily a tall order, since securing camps is clearly in the interests of host governments and is already on the policy agendas of both host governments and UNHCR (see, for example, the discussion concerning UNHCR's Convention Plus[4]).

A second component necessary for ensuring safety and dignity is freedom of movement and the right to work, as stated in the 1951 Convention (Articles 17,18, 19, and 26). While designated areas can be required places of residence for refugees, they should not be places to which refugees are restricted. It is very important that refugees are permitted to move freely in and out of their areas to engage in economic and social activities, including work, and to make use of services in the host community. Not all refugees will take advantage of this freedom, and so-called "vulnerables"—such as children and the aged infirm—will need assistance in the camp. But most adults want to pursue their own livelihoods, and the freedom to do so will ensure that refugee areas do not sink into places of squalor, inactivity, and dependence on relief.

In advocating the right to work, two concerns on the part of host governments need to be addressed. One is the fear that refugees will increase competition for jobs where there is already high unemployment. This is a long-standing and well-entrenched issue in countries of in-migration and cannot be dismissed easily. Clearly if refugees are allowed to work, they will compete for jobs. While this is in the interests of employers and possibly the local economy, it is not in the interests of local workers. Attempts to protect local workers are not helped by restricting refugees to camps. However, unless camps are made into prisons, refugees will move out of them to engage in economic activities. If this movement constitutes breaking the law, refugees outside camps will be moving in an illegal space. They will require more policing and will be at further risk for harassment and even engagement with other criminal activities. By contrast, if their movement is legal, they will require less policing and are more likely to enter the formal sector and pay taxes. In addition, as discussed in earlier chapters, there is now growing evidence of the economic and social contribution refugees can make to host areas through their entrepreneurial, farming, and livestock skills and by virtue of the increased economic activity in rural and urban areas. This contribution can at least help to offset concerns about competition.

There is also evidence that asylum-seekers, particularly those in urban areas, *create* employment.[5] Generally urban asylum-seekers are better educated than their rural counterparts and sometimes have higher education and skill levels compared with nationals of the host country.[6] If they were allowed to use their education and skills, the economic benefits to the host country would outweigh the costs of competition. Forward-thinking governments who recognize and seek to take advantage of urban refugees' human capital might consider locating designated zones close to cities. This would ensure a secure place of residence for asylum-seekers, who could then work in the city.

A second concern on the part of host governments is that the right to work will act as a magnet for migrants posing as asylum-seekers. This concern is also a real one, but the European Council on Refugees and Exiles (ECRE) argues that the significance of the right to work is often exaggerated as a "pull-factor" attracting asylum-seekers: "Given the ease with which illegal migrants find work on the black market in both western and non-western countries, it is unlikely that those whose sole motivation is to find work would bother to make an asylum claim, thereby attracting the attention of the authorities."[7] ECRE goes on to argue that it is wise to allow asylum-seekers access to the labor market, as "many asylum-seekers are genuine refugees and will be allowed to remain: an early opportunity to seek employment will help their eventual integration into their host society." The right to freedom of movement and to work must be supported by the provision of adequate and timely documentation, especially identity documents that are widely recognized, but also travel documents that enable asylum-seekers to cross borders. This provision is part of the process of treating asylum-seekers as legal denizens of the host country and removing the quasi-legal status many of them cope with under current conditions. This requirement is clearly stated for refugees in the 1951 Convention (Articles 25, 26, and 27) and should be extended to asylum-seekers. In the designated zone, a branch of the host government's refugees department could be set up, and the documentation needs of asylum-seekers would then be easier to fulfill compared with having a central office in the capital to which asylum-seekers must find their way, which is the case in most countries.

A final ingredient in ensuring refugees' safety and dignity is the right to stay in the host country and not be pressured to repatriate. Offering the option of citizenship to refugees who have lived as law-abiding denizens for a requisite period of time is laudable on the part of governments. But citizenship should not be required as long as refugees are allowed to live with a degree of dignity and security, at least at the level of their host community.[8]

Principle III: Doing Away with Parallel Services

Refugee assistance can be divided into two types of services: those that are specialized to address the needs of forcibly displaced people (including emergency shelter, emergency health and nutrition services, trauma counseling, family tracing, and legal aid) and those that are needed by both refugees and the host community (including education, health services, and agricultural support services). Most specialized services are particularly needed during or soon after an emergency influx, but some continue to be required over time—for example, family tracing or special nutrition requirements. As the emergency phase passes and refugees becomes more settled, other services of the type needed by all communities become equally important, but, as discussed earlier, humanitarian assistance funds are often restricted to refugees, even in host situations of widespread poverty and deprivation. Relief agencies provide schools, clinics, and economic stimulus packages for refugees, but these services are underfunded in the local community. In particular, when livelihood programs—which are a form of economic stimulus packages and can include agricultural or pastoralist extension services, seeds and tools, income generating projects, vocational training, and microfinance—are provided to refugees by humanitarian agencies, they are rarely extended to the host community. The resulting system of parallel services is both unfair and inequitable and is not in the interests of refugees in the long run. When refugees receive a disproportionate number or level of services relative to the host community, the resulting resentment on the part of the local community will render refugees less able to pursue independent livelihoods because they will confront obstacles created by both the local community and local authorities. The argument for integrating assistance for both refugees and nationals is thus based on fairness and on political expediency.

In recent years there have been calls for the abolishment of the traditional parallel systems,[9] but efforts to do so are confronted by significant institutional obstacles. First, host governments are heavily invested, both bureaucratically and in terms of aid flows, in retaining traditional relief models based on parallel systems. Separate government agencies or even departments are established to handle refugee affairs. These departments frequently replicate the tasks of other ministries, such as Health, Water, and Education, but depend on international aid for funding for refugees. International funding streams, particularly those of UNHCR and the United States, are mostly aimed at "care and maintenance" regimes in camps.[10] Spending on refugees outside of camps in countries of first asylum is miniscule. Since the existence of camps is the reason for inflows of humanitarian assistance, governments retain the camp model and the parallel system persists.

International aid agencies, like host governments, are also heavily invested in retaining traditional relief models, particularly when these mean that resources are transferred through them and expertise comes from them. Most refugee assistance is oriented around the emergency phase, when international agencies with relevant technical expertise are brought in to deal with emergency needs. These agencies have their own bureaucracies in place and it is more efficient to use them rather than try to integrate with existing government agencies. While this approach is perhaps valid during an emergency, over the long run, when integration with government or local agencies and services is feasible, there are no incentives for international aid agencies to shift aid delivery and implementation to local government agencies. Common reasons given for this reluctance are the corruption of local government departments, the lack of capacity and expertise of local agencies, and the lack of neutrality and risk of ethnic/political favoritism on the part of local governments or agencies. However, international aid agencies are by no means free of corruption and other vices, nor are they necessarily better equipped with expertise to implement local programs compared with local agencies. The difficulties of overcoming parallel systems cannot be dismissed, but efforts are being made in some countries.

Past and Present Examples of Host Countries that Approach the Proposed Model

The principles discussed in the previous section are based on rights enshrined in the 1951 Convention and other international instruments, but relatively few host governments have inscribed them in national refugee law and policy or otherwise implemented them. Most host governments are reluctant to do so because they fear opening the door to full integration, which is a politically unpopular prospect at present. However, a number of countries of first asylum, including Côte d'Ivoire, Sierra Leone, Mozambique, Uganda, Guinea, and Zambia, have implemented host policies that include components of the model proposed here. Recently, however, many of these governments have rescinded the more liberal aspects of their policies, especially the right to freedom of movement, and now require refugees to live in camps. Three examples of host countries whose refugee policies approximate the kind of approach advocated here are discussed below. As in most counties of first asylum, very few of the refugees have formal status, since the government's determination procedures are heavily backlogged, so most are technically asylum-seekers, or *prima facie* refugees. For convenience, we will refer to them simply as refugees.

Zambia's Western Province

Since independence in 1964, Zambia has been a generous host to refugees from most of its neighboring countries, including South Africa, Zimbabwe, Mozambique, and Zaire (now the Democratic Republic of Congo). The biggest "case load" has always been Angolan refugees, who began entering Zambia's western and north-western provinces after 1966, when the revolt against Portuguese colonial rule spread to the east of Angola and then developed into full-scale civil war after the Portuguese left in 1975.[11] In 1971, the Refugee (Control) Act was passed in Zambia, which required that all refugees live in an area designated by the government unless they received special permission to live elsewhere. Most Angolans are *prima facie* refugees and do not have formal Convention status. Until 2000, rather than camps, Zambia pursued a policy of settlements, in which refugee households were allocated land for cultivation and expected to produce their own food. But very large numbers of refugees also become self-settled and have never registered with the authorities. They live mostly in rural areas near the border with Angola, but an unknown number, possibly in the thousands, has moved to urban areas, where they live illegally and without permission to work or receive official assistance.

A small number of well-educated refugees from urban backgrounds have permission to stay in the urban areas, where they can practice their skills. By 2004, there were approximately 132,000 mainly Angolan refugees in Zambia's western province; roughly 22,000 lived in the settlement at Mayukwayukwa (set up in 1966), some 25,000 lived in two camps near Nangweshi (set up in 2000),[12] and an estimated 85,000 refugees were self-settled.

The Zambian policy response demonstrates many positive features. In the designated area of residence, refugees are given access to land and are permitted freedom of movement. Refugees must get permission from the Refugee Officer to leave the camps,[13] but this is a relatively simple matter, and refugees are rarely turned down. Most reasons for leaving are accepted, including visiting relatives, trading, or doing "piecework" on Zambian farms. Many people leave the camps without permission, and although they risk arrest, few refugees who move about outside the camps report government harassment or any security problems.[14] Refugees can thus pursue livelihoods on a par with the local Zambians, given that the western province region is the poorest and least developed part of Zambia. Zambian policy has some weaknesses, particularly relating to urban refugees, but also to the lack of provision for refugees who were born and raised in Zambia to become Zambian citizens. In addition, most services to refugees are provided through a parallel system, with separate schools and clinics for refugees in the camp at Nangweshi and little involvement at the local level.

By 1998, the history of failed peace efforts in Angola meant there had been many failed attempts at repatriation coupled with new outflows. In this context of protracted stay and parallel systems of assistance coupled with low likelihood of repatriation, an interesting experiment was conceived by the government, UNHCR, and donors. The Zambia Initiative was a project that recognized the refugees as "agents of development" for the region and sought to integrate them into their host communities. The government called it a "Development through Local Integration (DLI) project that promotes a holistic approach in addressing the needs of refugee hosting areas." Its main objective is "to alleviate the combined effects of food deficit, poor infrastructure, limited access to public services and economic opportunities, and in the process [find] durable solutions for refugees."[15]

The Zambia Initiative was officially launched by a donor mission in March 2002. In February 2002 the death of the UNITA leader, Jonas Savimbi, led to the end of the war in Angola, and after mid-2002, the assumption of non-repatriation was no longer valid. However, repatriation was slow to get started as refugees waited to see whether peace would hold, and although by 2004 many had started to return and a repatriation program was in place, at present it is likely that many refugees will remain in Zambia, where they have become settled after many years of residence. Thus the Zambia Initiative is still in place and is now in its second year of operation. The project supports agriculture credit, animal draft, construction and infrastructure development, and some health and education projects in the refugee-affected areas of the western province, in particular around Mayukwayukwa and Nangweshi. Although it is still too soon for an impact assessment, the Zambia Initiative is an interesting example of a development project that incorporates locals and refugees, and could be a model for other protracted refugee situations.

Mozambique

Since the early 1990s, when its own civil war ended, Mozambique has hosted over 10,000 refugees, mostly Congolese, but with significant populations of Burundians and Rwandans and small numbers of other nationalities.[16] During the 1990s most refugees lived in and around the capital city of Maputo, but in 2001, the government and UNCHR decided to relocate all refugees to Nampula, a city approximately 2,000 km north of Maputo, where a new camp was constructed.[17] This voluntary relocation took place in 2003, and by mid-2004, there were over 5,000 refugees living in Maratane Refugee Camp, 20 km from Nampula, with an average of 100 to 120 new arrivals each month, mostly from the Democratic Republic of the Congo. Since the relocation, all refugees are required to live in the Nampula region unless they have authorization by the government.[18] If refugees choose to live outside the camp, they no longer receive assistance from the government or UNHCR. Today roughly 2,500 urban refugees live in Maputo, and another 1,500 or so refugees live in other towns, including Nampula.

Refugees have freedom of movement and can leave and enter Maratane camp as they please. As in Zambia, they must state the length of time they will be away from the camp and their reasons for traveling, and the government grants permission according to time allotments of 24, 48, and 72 hours. (Under pressure from the refugees, the camp administration is considering extending the time for up to seven days.) The land surrounding the camp is loaned to international aid agency World Relief, for their agricultural program, and refugees have access to that land by participating in the program. Refugee children attend local schools and pay the same school fees as Mozambicans. There is a Mozambican primary school in the camp, mostly attended by local Mozambican children, and the secondary school is in Nampula, which means refugee families must pay for their children's transportation there.

Refugees have the right to work in Mozambique and are encouraged to work by both the UNCHR and the government. Skilled refugees, including teachers and nurses, are recruited by the government to work in the more remote regions of Mozambique, where there are shortages of skilled Mozambicans. The Ministry of Education provides equivalency paperwork for professionals and those with university degrees. For other refugees, high unemployment makes it difficult to find work outside the camp. Employers are reluctant to hire refugees because they are unsure of their documentation or their legal status. There is no proper work in the camp other than petty trade, but if refugees leave the camp to open shops and live in Nampula, they are cut off from UNCHR assistance and food distribution. While this would not be a problem if they could make a go of their businesses, urban refugees experience problems. Many complain of discrimination and harassment by both governmental officials and local shop owners, and some report having had their stores or homes robbed or destroyed.

In terms of the right to work, freedom of movement, and access to local services, Mozambican refugee policy is relatively progressive, although refugees encounter obstacles and bureaucratic problems, in particular difficulties with documentation requirements. The permit known as the *Declaração*, which allows registered asylum-seekers to live in Mozambique, requires renewal every two months. This renewal process is burdensome, as it requires travel to Maputo (a distance of 2,000 km) and long waits at the government office.

Insofar as providing a secure environment for refugees, the Mozambican government and UNHCR have had less success. In Maratane camp, security problems usually stem from within the Congolese community. The ethnic tensions and violence that caused people to flee the DRC have been replicated in the camp, and ethnic minorities and vulnerable women are often targets for violence and threats. Refugees of different nationalities, including Rwandans and Burundians, are marginalized and targeted by the Congolese. Camp security is organized by the government, but it is under-resourced, and camp residents said they do not feel protected by the policemen, who do nothing when crimes are reported.[19] A community security force paid by UNCHR has had more success in the camp and is seen as flexible and able to solve internal disputes. Outside the camp there are fewer security problems. There are good relations between camp residents and the local Mozambican villagers who live close to the camp and frequently trade with each other. Urban refugees, however, seem to encounter more problems, including harassment, perhaps because they are seen as competitors with local merchants. The scope of these security problems is difficult to ascertain without further research. Ensuring the security of refugees is an endemic problem in Mozambique, as it is in most countries of first asylum.

Sierra Leone

In mid-2004 Sierra Leone was in its fourth year of peace and at the end of a huge repatriation of both refugees and IDPs from its long war. At the same time, since late 2002, it had hosted thousands of Liberian refugees, many living in eight refugee camps in or near the eastern city of Kenema, the third largest city in Sierra Leone, approximately 60 km from the Liberian border. These Liberian refugees had either fled directly to Sierra Leone when the killings of civilians increased in Liberia, or they had been relocated from camps in Guinea when security problems there escalated.[20] As of March 2004 there were almost 55,000 refugees living in the eight camps, and over 5,000 refugees in urban areas of Sierra Leone who do not get food assistance. Sierra Leoneans also live in the camps, sometimes moving into the abandoned houses of refugees who returned to Liberia. Like the Angolan refugees in Zambia, the Liberian refugees are watching the situation in their home country, waiting for the election to see whether peace will hold there and they can safely repatriate.

In Sierra Leone, the Liberian refugees have many rights, including freedom of movement; the ability to work; and access to land, schools, and social services within the camp. The refugees walk to the market or to neighboring villages for daily contract work. Those with businesses and money for transportation travel to the towns of Bo and Kenema and even as far as Freetown to buy and sell goods. Some refugees also use their freedom of movement to cross the border to Liberia to check on their homes and family members and then return to the camps in Sierra Leone. Relations with the host communities are perceived as good. Few problems with the local citizens are reported, and there is even some sympathy on the part of Sierra Leoneans: one Liberian woman business owner said that she got out of paying a bribe when she showed the policeman her ration card. The refugees are able to work daily contracts for people in the host community, including weeding, "brushing" farms (preparing the land for cultivation), cutting wood, washing clothes, or hauling large planks of wood from the bush to the roadside. Refugees usually get paid less than the citizens for this work. Inside the camps, there is occasional contract work—such as ditchdigging, construction, or weeding—which pays somewhat higher wages. Many refugees said they could not get valued work with NGOs because of their low education levels; the NGOs only hired people with high levels of education.

Refugees live in the camp, but they are quite easily able to gain access to land to farm or cut wood or grass in the bush. Permission must be obtained from the host community, which UNCHR helps negotiate. Most refugees who want to farm are able to do so, and in mid-2004 the farms were doing well, and people were waiting until the harvest before moving back to Liberia. As in Mozambique and Zambia, services for refugees tend towards the parallel system, with primary schools in the camps, and secondary school-age children going to the local schools without paying fees. Three of the camps have health clinics and in the fourth, the refugees go to the health clinic in the host community free of charge, except for the cost of medicine.

Unlike Maratane camp in Mozambique, but like the Zambian camps and settlements, the Sierra Leonean camps have, for the most part, escaped the problem of insecurity. Most people agreed that there was almost no violent conflict and tensions and—except for one camp, Tobanda, which has experienced a crime wave—people think crime has decreased since their arrival. Local police patrol the camps during the day, and refugees trained as Camp Wardens guard the camp at night. Crimes are brought before the camp's grievance committee, which decides on the case or forwards it to the police.

Applying the Case Studies to the Model

Although the host situations are not perfect in any of the three countries discussed, and there is some concern that the governments might implement more restrictions in the near future, they demonstrate ways in which refugees can live in relative security and dignity. This does not mean that all the refugees are self-sufficient or no longer in need of aid (although some are); indeed, many of the host countries' own citizens live in dire poverty. But the refugees have been afforded some modicum of security and dignity and given the chance to pursue livelihoods if they so desire. In each of the examples, refugees are required to live in designated zones, but they have freedom of movement, both within and outside of the zone and further afield. They are able to engage in economic activities, including employment, trade, and farming, and they live in relative security. There are problems that persist, however. When designated zones are in remote or rural areas, those who are from urban backgrounds cannot survive with dignity and move to urban areas. Urban refugees who lack the skills and education that will get them permission to work must try to survive without any assistance from aid agencies and often with harassment of varying degrees from the authorities. The problem of urban refugees is a growing one, with few viable solutions given host governments' reluctance to allow refugees to live where they choose.

All three of the countries discussed issue refugees permits or identity documents of some sort, but, as in many countries of first asylum, their administrative apparatus is in some disarray, not working well, and heavily backlogged. There are several common problems:

- The system cannot process refugees fast enough, so refugees lack the necessary identification documents;
- Asylum-seekers have to renew their ID too frequently, and this creates a significant resource burden (transportation costs, lost time, and fees);
- Government officials, police, and other authorities are not familiar with the different forms of refugee documentation and do not recognize refugee identification.

These bureaucratic obstacles are unnecessary and perhaps unintended hindrances to refugees' ability to pursue livelihoods. They could be relatively easily addressed with improved systems and training of officials. However, doing so requires political will on the part of host governments, and refugees often are not a high priority. This is where donors can apply pressure—in the form of conditionality —to ensure that measures are taken to improve bureaucracies before funding is forthcoming.

In terms of efforts to address parallel systems, only Zambia, through the Zambia Initiative, appears to be trying to integrate refugees with the host community through provision of needed economic inputs. However, Zambia, like most host countries, including Sierra Leone and Mozambique, continues to separate most services for refugees from the host community, although some effort has been made to integrate school systems.

Making the Model Work

A refugee policy based on providing asylum-seekers with a designated area of residence where they have rights, security, and a dignified way to pursue a livelihood is a feasible and politically viable option for countries of first asylum in the developing world. Such a policy will require the advocacy of donors and aid agencies. It will also require continued international presence in designated refugee areas, both to ensure that specialized refugee services are provided for those who need them and to promote protection of refugees' economic and social rights.

Refugees' rights and obligations are all clearly stated in the Articles of the 1951 Convention, but they have not been widely implemented in the national refugee legislation of many host countries. Working with host countries to bring about refugee legislation is one aspect of UNHCR's mandate, and these advocacy efforts are assisted by various NGOs in host countries. Similarly, the call for the abolishment of parallel systems is increasingly widespread, again with little progress except in a small number of cases. Advocacy efforts to promote these changes can be boosted if donors add some conditionality to their provision of humanitarian assistance. Before humanitarian assistance is forthcoming, donors can require host governments to implement security measures and assign asylum-seekers their economic rights. These requirements should go beyond broad statements and should be spelled out in jointly agreed activities, such as specific measures taken to ensure security, which should be verified before aid disbursements are made.

In turn, host governments can require that donors and international organizations put a plan in place for burden-sharing arrangements that do away with parallel systems of services. This will be a challenge, given how parallel systems are currently entrenched in the *modus operandi* and ideologies of most aid agencies, not to mention bureaucratic inertia. However, in protracted situations where emergency needs are less pressing and levels of humanitarian assistance are declining, it might be possible to come up with new ways of providing assistance that include the host communities. As aid agencies become less able to provide for refugees, refugees will need to rely on their own economic activities in the local community. Refugees will be less able to function in host communities where there is local resentment and antagonism stemming from the host community's perception that refugees have received unfair advantages from humanitarian agencies. When UNHCR tries to push local integration on a host community that is already resentful about refugees receiving all the resources, it is too late. This is what happened in Côte d'Ivoire after 1997, when, according to Tom Kuhlman, the funds available for the refugees who did not repatriate to Liberia decreased sharply, and there were reduced "care and maintenance" handouts, such as food and free medical care. UNHCR then began to pursue local integration for the refugees, but Côte d'Ivoire was coping with economic decline and with "ominous ethnic tensions, strongly reducing its willingness to integrate refugees locally. The result of all this is that the outlook for local integration is far less favourable than before."[21]

To increase the likelihood that refugees will be well-received and able to function economically in the local community, UNHCR should work with the host government *from the start of a refugee operation* to provide education, health, and economic stimulus packages to the host community that refugees will also use. In putting together country programs for refugees, aid agencies should ensure that budgets offset the burden of refugees on the social services of host communities and include compensation for the additional costs for a fixed number of years. Kuhlman suggests six years after the end of the mass inflow as adequate. "Care and maintenance" programs should be of limited duration, perhaps no more than one year, and refugee farmers should be assisted for only one or two seasons from the time they are first able to plant, unless local farmers also receive additional assistance. Further, the host community and host government can be encouraged to accept refugees by helping communities address environmental or other problems that might stem from the presence of refugees. If UNHCR cannot do this itself, it should take the lead in encouraging other organizations like the UN Environmental Program and UNDP to get involved.[22]

Specialized services for refugees, including those defined as "vulnerables," should be handled with great care and with plenty of local input. Where public goods are provided to certain categories of people, others will try to pass for those categories to gain access to the goods. This is true of all public goods, whether we are talking about asylum, corporate tax breaks, or welfare. It is also true of food aid and other humanitarian resources, including resettlement. When these goods are only available to so-called "vulnerable groups" in refugee camps and settlements, other "non-vulnerables"—both refugees and nationals—will be tempted to exhibit vulnerability so as to pass as refugees and gain access to those resources. Gaim Kibreab says it is possible "to look at such behaviour as acts of defiance against the vague and often subjective criteria used by aid agencies to divide people into separate categories, e.g. vulnerable (deserving), non-vulnerable (non-deserving), internally displaced persons, local residents, refugees and returnees."[23] The definition of who is vulnerable should incorporate local criteria and the advice of the local community, which should be asked to identify such individuals. Services for vulnerables should be carefully designed, using local guidance, and should not be blanket approaches that last indefinitely.

Several enabling factors will contribute to the success of a policy that allows refugees to pursue livelihoods in host communities. When refugees share language, culture, or ethnic origin with the host community, they are more likely to be welcomed and assisted. When refugees are perceived as hard workers, or when they bring particular skills, resources (including humanitarian ones) and investments to their country of asylum, they will be welcomed. In host areas where there is land available, refugees are more likely to be allowed to move around freely. The presence of these factors should be seen as opportunities for donors and aid agencies to promote livelihood opportunities for refugees.

Conclusion

If refugee situations were temporary and of short duration, it would make sense for assistance to be focused on repatriation. Refugees could be separated from their host society and provided for by international relief agencies in temporary camps, their children educated in the curriculum of their home countries and their impact on the host country minimized. But by now we know better than to believe that civil wars and intra-state conflict will be of limited duration. Where any such situations have occurred—perhaps Kosovo is one example—they are the exception. Most refugee situations last well beyond the emergency period and, in many cases, permanent repatriation does not occur for many years. Yet aid operations and refugee policies continue to be built around the notion of temporariness and rapid repatriation. This book has drawn on the research and thinking of many observers to argue that we should direct refugee policies and assistance programs towards granting refugees their economic rights and enabling them to pursue livelihoods. In my view, this is more important than providing food aid and other handouts, targeting vulnerables, and pushing human rights—all projects which currently garner significant support (and resources) in the West but are less salient in refugee camps of long standing, where more urgent needs are pressing. All of these worthy goals can best be achieved when refugees are enabled to support themselves. They will then be better positioned to help their own communities—including the vulnerable—to mobilize to claim their human rights and seek justice and to gather themselves for repatriation.

Notes

1   In addition to more restrictions on asylum-seekers already in host countries, these measures include obstacles to entry, such as airline carrier sanctions; onerous visa requirements, including transit visas; and bilateral agreements with sending countries, such as readmission agreements. For more, see Crisp and Dessalegne, "Refugee Protection."

2   Article 9, "Provisional Measures," states that "Nothing in this Convention shall prevent a Contracting State, in time of war or other grave and exceptional circumstances, from taking provisionally measures which it considers to be essential to the national security in the case of a particular person, pending a determination by the Contracting State that that person is in fact a refugee and that the continuance of such measures is necessary in his case in the interests of national security."

3   There is now a considerable literature on refugees' experience in camps. For recent interesting perspectives, see Hoeing, "Self-Image"; Cindy Horst, "Vital Links in Social Security: Somali Refugees in the Dadaab Camps, Kenya," (working paper, New Issues in Refugee Research, no. 38, UNHCR, 2001); Kibreab, "Pulling Wool," 1-26; Stefan Sperl, "International Refugee Aid and Social Change in Northern Mali," (working paper, New Issues in Refugee Research, no. 22, UNHCR, 2000).

4   Documentation on the Convention Plus can be found at www.unhcr.ch/cgi-bin/texis/vtx/home?page=PROTECT&id=406d21802&ID=406d21802&PUBLISHER=TWO.

5 See, for example, Dryden-Peterson and Hovil, "Local Integration" for urban refugees in Kampala; Landau and Jacobsen, "Refugees in New Johannesburg," 44-46 for Johannesburg.

6 As discussed in Chapter Three, there is some evidence that their overall education and skills levels are higher than those of natives.

7 See the European Council on Refugees and Exiles (ECRE) Web site at www.ecre.org/factfile/facts.shtml#12.

8 Jeff Crisp, "The Local Integration and Local Settlement of Refugees: A Conceptual and Historical Analysis," (working paper, New Issues in Refugee Research, no. 102, UNHCR, 2004), 3.

9 See, for example, Kuhlman, *Responding to Protracted Refugee Situations*; Merrill Smith, "Introduction to the World Refugee Survey," *World Refugee Survey, 2004* (Washington, DC: U.S. Committee for Refugees and Immigrants, 2004). www.refugees.org/wrs04/main.html.

10 Jacobsen, "Just Enough," 48.

11 Much of this case material is taken from Oliver Bakewell, "Review of CORD Community Services for Angolan Refugees in Western Province, Zambia," UNHCR EPAU/2002/14 (2002), and from Sarah Titus, *CORD Microcredit Programs for Refugees, Nangweshi, Zambia,* Alchemy Project Country Report No. 8, August 2004, available at www.famine.tufts.edu/pdf/.alchemy/2004_8_zambia.pdf. Material is also taken from the Zambia Initiative reports, put out jointly by UNHCR and the Government of Zambia available on the UNHCR Web site (www.unhcr.ch).

12 In the case of Nangweshi, according to Bakewell, the government would prefer a settlement rather than a camp and has sought to relocate the refugees to an area where they could have land for cultivation, but it has not been possible to find a piece of land that is acceptable to the area's traditional rulers, the Lozi chiefs. See Bakewell, "Review," 10.

13 Each of the settlements and camps is presided over by a Refugee Officer from the Commissioner of Refugees within the Ministry of Home Affairs who has authority over everyone working or living in the camp.

14 See Bakewell, "Review," 10. The author's own interviews with refugees at Nangweshi confirm this.

15 Government of Zambia and UNHCR, "Zambia Initiative: In Pursuit"; "Zambia Initiative: Refugee-Hosting"; "Zambia Initiative: Development through Local Integration—Programme Formulation Mission" (October 6–13, 2002); all available at www.unchr.ch.

16 Much of this section draws on Anna Mecagni, *World Relief's Income Generation Animal Husbandry Program, Maratane Refugee Camp, Mozambique,* Alchemy Project Country Report No. 5, August 2004; available at www.famine.tufts.edu/work/refugees.html.

17   The government justified this move by stating that it did not want refugees in the capital city because they caused problems and confusion. However, it has been suggested that the relocation decision arose because of pressure from the South African government, which sought to reduce the refugees' proximity to the border of South Africa. Mecagni, "World Relief's Income," 1.

18   Some refugees, particularly those who were small business owners or relatively better off, chose to remain in Maputo, where the government later provided them with official permission to remain. The government agency responsible for refugees, Instituto Nacional de Apoio aos Refugiados (INAR), is also UNHCR's implementing partner.

19   According to Mecagni, fourteen policemen are stationed at the camp, ten of whom were formerly retired and have been called back to service. They do not wear uniforms, except for the police commander and the chief of police. Equipment is limited—they do not have radios, for example—which makes logistics and overall security work difficult. Some policemen have poor vision and alcohol problems. However, it is difficult to derive a complete picture of security at the camp. As in most camps in countries of first asylum, many refugees are seeking resettlement and there is a common belief that if you are a camp resident with security problems (e.g., a target of crime or violence), you are more likely to be resettled. Some therefore suspect that some of the crimes committed at the camp may be fabricated for resettlement purposes. Mecagni, "World Relief's Income," 6.

20   Material from this section is taken largely from Elizabeth Buckius, *ARC Income Generation Projects for Liberian Refugees in Kenema, Sierra Leone*, Alchemy Project Country Report No. 1, August 2004; available at www.famine.tufts.edu/work/refugees.html.

21   Kuhlman, *Responding to Protracted Refugee Situations*, 4.

22   Kuhlman, *Responding to Protracted Refugee Situations*, 5.

23   Kibreab, "Pulling Wool," 18.

BIBLIOGRAPHY

Ahmed, Ismail. "Remittances and Their Economic Impact in Post-War Somaliland." *Disasters* 24 (2000): 380–89.

Akuei, Stephanie Riak. *Remittances as Unforeseen Burdens: Considering Displacement, Family and Resettlement Contexts in Refugee Livelihood and Well Being. Is There Anything States or Organisations Can Do?* UNHCR Evaluation and Policy Unit Background Document (May 2004). www.unhcr.ch.

Alchemy Project Annual Report 2002. Alchemy Project. Feinstein International Famine Center, Tufts University, Medford, MA. www.famine.tufts.edu/index .html?id=18.

Anderson, Mary B. *Do No Harm: How Aid Can Support Peace—Or War.* Boulder, CO: Lynne Rienner Publishers, Inc., 1999.

Andrews, B. Lacey. *When Is a Refugee Not a Refugee? Refugee/Host Relations in Guinea,* report no. 88, UNHCR Evaluation and Policy Analysis Unit (EPAU) Series, 2003.

Bakewell, Oliver. "Repatriation and Self-Settled Refugees in Zambia: Bringing Solutions to the Wrong Problems." *Journal of Refugee Studies* 13, no. 4 (2000): 256–373.

———. *Review of CORD Community Services for Angolan Refugees in Western Province, Zambia.* Report for UNHCR Evaluation and Policy Unit EPAU/ 2002/14, 2002.

Bascom, Jonathan. *Losing Place: Refugee Populations and Rural Transformations in East Africa.* New York: Berghahn Books, 1998.

———. "The New Nomads: An Overview of Involuntary Migration in Africa" in *The Migration Experience in Africa,* edited by Jonathan Baker and Tade Akin Aina, 187–219. Uppsala, Sweden: Nordiska Afrikainstitutet, 1995.

Belvedere, F., Z. Kimmie, and E. Mogodi. *National Refugee Baseline Survey: Final Report.* Community Agency for Social Enquiry, Japan International Cooperation, and UNHCR, 2003.

Blume, Karen. Immigrants and Low-Income in Denmark—Is Self-Employment Associated with an Upward Income Mobility? Paper presented at the WIDER Conference on Poverty, International Migration and Asylum, Helsinki, September 27–28, 2002. www.wider.unu.edu/conference/conference-2002-3/ conference-2002-3-papers.htm.

Buckius, Elizabeth. *ARC Income Generation Projects for Liberian Refugees in Kenema, Sierra Leone.* Alchemy Project Country Report No. 1, August 2004. www .famine.tufts.edu/work/refugees.html.

Callamard, Agnes. "Refugees and Local Hosts: A Study of the Trading Interactions between Mozambican Refugees and Malawian Villagers." *Journal of Refugee Studies* 7, no. 1 (1994): 23.

Carswell, Grace. "Livelihood Diversification in Southern Ethiopia." Working paper, no. 117, Institute of Development Studies, 2000.

Cernea, M. "The Risks and Reconstruction Model for Resettling Displaced Populations." *World Development* 25 (1997): 1569–87.

Christian Outreach for Relief and Development (CORD). *Self Reliance in Nyarugusu and Lugufu Camp with Congolese Refugees, Kasulu District, Western Tanzania.* Internal report. Lemington Spa, UK: CORD, 2003.

Crisp, Jeff. "The Local Integration and Local Settlement of Refugees: A Conceptual and Historical Analysis." Working paper, New Issues in Refugee Research, no. 102, UNHCR, 2004.

———. "No Solutions in Sight: The Problem of Protracted Refugee Situations in Africa." Working paper, New Issues in Refugee Research, no. 75, UNHCR, 2002.

Crisp, Jeff, and Damtew Dessalegne. "Refugee Protection and Migration Management: The Challenge for UNHCR." Working paper, New Issues in Refugee Research, no. 64, UNHCR, 2002.

Crush, Jonathan. "The Dark Side of Democracy: Migration, Human Rights and Xenophobia in South Africa." *International Migration* no. 38 (2000): 103–34.

De Haan, A. "Livelihoods and Poverty: The Role of Migration—A Critical Review of the Migration Literature." *The Journal of Development Studies* 36 (1999): 1–47.

Dent, John A. "Research Paper on the Social and Economic Rights of Non-Nationals in Europe." European Council on Refugees and Exiles (ECRE) Commissioned Research Paper, 2002. www.ecre.org/research/socecon.pdf.

Dick, Shelly. "Liberians in Ghana: Living without Humanitarian Assistance." Working paper, New Issues in Refugee Research, no. 57, UNHCR, 2002.

———. "Review of CORD Community Services for Congolese Refugees in Tanzania" EPAU/2002/13 (December 2002): 4. www.unhcr.ch/cgi-bin/texis/vtx/home?page=search.

Doyle, Karen. "Microfinance in the Wake of Conflict: Challenges and Opportunities." The SEEP Network, 1998. www.usaid.gov/our_work/cross-cutting _programs/conflict/publications/other_usaid.html.

Dryden-Peterson, Sarah, and Lucy Hovil. "Local Integration as a Durable Solution: Refugees, Host Populations and Education in Uganda." Working paper, New Issues in Refugee Research, no. 93, UNHCR, 2003.

Duffield, Mark. "Shifting Sands: The Search for 'Coherence' between Political and Humanitarian Responses to Complex Emergencies." Humanitarian Policy Group Report 8. London: ODI, August 2001.

Ellis, S., and S. Barakat. "From Relief to Development: The Long-term Effects of 'Temporary' Accommodation of Refugees and Displaced Persons in the Republic of Croatia." *Disasters* 20 (1996): 111–24.

Eyber, Carola. *FMO Research Guide: Psychosocial Issues* (October 2002). Forced Migration Online, www.forcedmigration.org/guides/fmo004.

Flowers, Jeff. "Microfinance and Internally Displaced Persons in Azerbaijan." Paper for UNHCR Refugees Livelihood Network, FINCA Azerbaijan, November 21, 2003. www.unhcr.ch.

Gammage, Sarah, and Jorge Fernandez, "Conflict, Displacement and Reintegration: Household Survey Evidence from El Salvador." Working paper, New Issues in Refugee Research, no. 25, UNHCR, 2000, 22.

Gammeltoft, Peter. "Remittances and Other Financial Flows to Developing Countries." Paper for the Migration-Development Links Project at the Danish Institute for International Studies, Copenhagen, 2002. www.cdr.dk/Res THEMES/conflict/migdevfinal.htm.

Goodhand, J., and D. Hulme. "Understanding Conflict and Peace-Building in the New World Disorder." *Third World Quarterly* 20, no. 1 (1999): 13–26.

Government of Uganda, and UNHCR. *Self Reliance Strategy (1999–2003) for Refugee Hosting Areas in Moyo, Aruna and Adjumani Districts, Uganda,* Report of the Midterm Review: RLSS Mission Report, April 2004. www.unhcr.ch.

Government of Zambia, and UNHCR. *Zambia Initiative: In Pursuit of Sustainable Solutions for Refugees in Zambia,* May 1, 2004.

Government of Zambia, and UNHCR. *Zambia Initiative: Development through Local Integration—Programme Formulation Mission,* October 6–13, 2002.

Government of Zambia, and UNHCR. *Zambia Initiative: Refugee-Hosting Community Development Programme.* Donors Mission Report, March 18–28, 2002.

Green, R. "Regaining and Securing Access to Common Property Resources," in *Risks and Reconstruction: Experiences of Resettlers and Refugees,* edited by Michael M. Cernea and Christopher McDowell, 253–290. Washington, DC: World Bank, 2000.

Groot, Fedde Jan, Deputy Representative to the United Nations High Commissioner for Refugees in South Africa, "UNHCR's Policy on Refugees in Urban Areas: The Case of South Africa," speech at University of the Witwatersrand, Johannesburg, April 30, 2003.

Hamid, G.M. "Livelihood Patterns of Displaced Households in Greater Khartoum." *Disasters* 16 (1992): 230–39.

Harrell-Bond, Barbara. Toward the Economic and Social "Integration" of Refugee Populations in Host Countries in Africa. Paper presented at a conference organized by the Stanley Foundation, "Refugee Protection in Africa: How to Ensure Security and Development for Refugees and Hosts," Entebbe, Uganda, November 2002.

Hendrickson, D., and J. Armon. "The Changing Nature of Conflict and Famine Vulnerability: The Case of Livestock Raiding in Turkana District, Kenya." *Disasters* 22 (1998): 185–99.

Hoeing, Wiebke. "Self-Image and the Well-Being of Refugees in Rhino Camp, Uganda." Working paper, New Issues in Refugee Research, no. 103, UNHCR, 2004.

Horst, Cindy. "Money and Mobility: Transnational Livelihood Strategies of the Somali Diaspora." *Global Migration Perspectives* no. 9 (October 2004). www.gcim.org/ir_gmp.htm.

Horst, Cindy. "Vital Links in Social Security: Somali Refugees in the Dadaab Camps, Kenya." Working paper, New Issues in Refugee Research, no. 38, UNHCR, 2001.

Horst, Cindy, and Nicholas Van Hear. "Counting the Cost: Refugees, Remittances and the 'War on Terrorism'." *Forced Migration Review* no. 14 (2002): 32–34.

Hovil, Lucy, and Alex Moorehead. "War as Normal: The Impact of Violence on the Lives of Displaced Communities Living in Pader District, Northern Uganda." Working paper, Refugee Law Project, no. 5, 2002.

Hovy, Bela. "Statistically Correct Asylum Data: Prospects and Limitations." Working paper, New Issues in Refugee Research, no. 37, UNHCR, 2001.

Hyndman, Jennifer, and B. Viktor Nylund. "UNHCR and the Status of Prima Facie Refugees in Kenya." *International Journal of Refugee Law* 10, no. 1/2 (1998): 21–48.

Jacobsen, Karen. "The Forgotten Solution: Local Integration for Refugees in Developing Countries." Working paper, New Issues in Refugee Research, no. 45, UNHCR, 2001.

———. "Just Enough for the City: Urban Refugees Make Their Own Way." *World Refugee Survey, 2004.* Washington, DC: U.S. Committee for Refugees and Immigrants. www.refugees.org/wrs04/main.html.

———. "Livelihoods in Conflict: The Pursuit of Livelihoods by Refugees and the Impact on the Human Security of Host Communities." Expert working paper prepared for the Center for Development Research Study: Migration-Development Links: Evidence and Options, February 2002.

———. "Supporting Displaced Livelihoods with Microcredit and Other Income Generating Programs: Findings from the Alchemy Project, 2001–2004." Feinstein International Famine Center, Tufts University, Medford, MA, November 2004. www.famine.tufts.edu.

Jacobsen, Karen, and Loren Landau. "The Dual Imperative in Refugee Research: Some Methodological and Ethical Considerations in Social Science Research on Forced Migration." *Disasters* 27, no. 3 (2003): 185–206.

Jacobsen, Karen, and Sarah Bailey. "Micro-Credit and Banking for Refugees in Johannesburg" in *Forced Migrants in the New Johannesburg: Towards a Local*

Government Response, edited by Loren Landau, 99–102. Johannesburg: Wits University, 2004.

Jamal, Arafat. *Minimum Standards and Essential Needs in a Protracted Refugee Situation. A review of the UNHCR Programme in Kakuma, Kenya.* Report for UNHCR Evaluation and Policy Unit EPAU/2000/05, November 2000. www.unhcr.ch/cgi-bin/texis/vtx/home/opendoc.pdf?tbl=RESEARCH&id =3ae6bd4c0&page=research.

Kaiser, Tania. *A Beneficiary-Based Evaluation of the UNHCR Programme in Guinea*, report for UNHCR Evaluation and Policy Analysis Unit, 2001.

———. "Participation, Self-Reliance and Integration: Sudanese Refugees in Uganda." *ID21 Insights* 44, December 2002. www.id21.org/insights/insights 44/insights-iss44-art04.html.

———. "Participatory and Beneficiary-Based Approaches to the Evaluation of Humanitarian Programmes." Working paper, New Issues in Refugee Research, no. 51, UNHCR, February 2002.

———. "UNHCR's Withdrawal from Kiryandongo: Anatomy of a Handover." Working paper, New Issues in Refugee Research, no. 32, UNHCR, 2000.

Karadawi, A. "The Problem of Urban Refugees in Sudan," in *Refugees: A Third World Dilemma*, edited by John Rogge. Totowa, NJ: Rowman & Littlefield, 1987.

Keen, D. "A Disaster for Whom? Local Interests and International Donors During Famine among the Dinka of Sudan." *Disasters* 15 (1991): 58–73.

Kibreab, Gaim. "Eritrean and Ethiopian Urban Refugees in Khartoum: What the Eye Refuses to See." *African Studies Review* 39, no. 3 (1996): 131–78.

———. "Pulling the Wool Over the Eyes of Strangers: Refugee Deceit and Trickery in Institutionalized Settings." *Journal of Refugee Studies* 14, no. 1 (2004): 1–26.

———. "Refugees in the Sudan: Unresolved Issues," in *African Refugees: Development Aid and Repatriation*, edited by Howard Adelman and John Sorenson, 43–68. Boulder, CO: Westview Press, 1994.

Koser, Khalid, and Nicholas Van Hear. "Asylum migration: implications for countries of origin." United Nations University/World Institute for Development Economics Research Discussion Paper DP 2003/20, February 2003.

Koser, Khalid, and Nadje Al-Ali, eds. *New Approaches to Migration? Transnational Communities and the Transformation of Home.* London: Routledge, 2001.

Kuhlman, Tom. *Burden or Boon? A Study of Eritrean Refugees in the Sudan* Amsterdam: V.U. Uitgeverij, 1990.

———. "Organized Versus Spontaneous Settlement of Refugees in Africa," in *African Refugees: Development Aid and Repatriation*, edited by Howard Adelman and John Sorenson, 117–142. Boulder, CO: Westview Press, 1994.

———. *Responding to Protracted Refugee Situations: A Case Study of Liberian Refugees in Côte d'Ivoire*, report for UNHCR Evaluation and Policy Unit, July 2002.

Landau, Loren. "Beyond the Losers: Transforming Governmental Practice in Refugee-Affected Tanzania." *Journal of Refugee Studies* 16, no. 1 (2003): 19–43.

———. FMO Research Guide: Study Guide to Urban Refugees (February 2004). Forced Migration Online. www.forcedmigration.org/guides/fmo024.

Landau, Loren, and Karen Jacobsen. "Refugees in the New Johannesburg." *Forced Migration Review* 19 (January 2004): 44–46.

Lautze, Sue, E. Stites, N. Nojumi, and F. Najimi. "Qaht-E-Pool 'A Cash Famine': Food Insecurity in Afghanistan 1999–2002." Working paper, Feinstein International Famine Center, October 28, 2002. www.famine.tufts.edu/pdf/cash _famine.pdf.

Macchiavello, Michela. "Forced Migrants as an Under-Utilized Asset: Refugee Skills, Livelihoods, and Achievements in Kampala, Uganda." Working paper, New Issues in Refugee Research, no. 95, UNHCR, 2003.

MacGaffey, Janet, and Remy Bazengguissa-Ganga. *Congo-Paris: Transnational Traders on the Margins of the Law.* Indiana: James Currey/Indiana University Press, 2000.

Macrae, Joanna, and Anthony Zwi, eds. *War and Hunger: Rethinking International Responses to Complex Emergencies.* With Mark Duffield and Hugo Slim. London: Zed Books in association with Save the Children Fund (UK), 1994.

Mecagni, Anna. *World Relief's Income Generation Animal Husbandry Program, Maratane Refugee Camp, Mozambique*, Alchemy Project Country Report No. 5, August 2004. www.famine.tufts.edu/work/refugees.html.

Miamidian, Eileen, and Karen Jacobsen. "Livelihood Interventions for Urban Refugees." Alchemy Project Workshop, Maputo, February 19–20, 2004. www .famine.tufts.edu.

Morarji, Maitri. "Alchemy Project Field Assessment: Arid Lands Development Focus, Wajir, Kenya." Alchemy Project Country Report No. 6, August 2004. www.famine.tufts.edu/pdf/alchemy/2004_6_kenya.pdf.

Morrison, John, and Beth Crosland. "The Trafficking and Smuggling of Refugees: The End Game in European Asylum Policy?" Working paper, New Issues in Refugee Research, no. 39, UNHCR, 2001.

Nourse, Timothy H. Microfinance for Refugees Emerging Principles for Effective Implementation. Paper for UNHCR Refugees Livelihood Network, ARC, 2003. www.unhcr.ch.

Ogden, K. "Coping Strategies Developed as a Result of Social Structure and Conflict: Kosovo in the 1990s." *Disasters* 24 (2000): 117–32.

Pain, Adam, and Sue Lautze. *Livelihoods in Afghanistan.* Kabul, Afghanistan: Afghanistan Research and Evaluation Unit, 2002.

Pérouse de Montclos, Marc-Antoine, and Peter Mwangi Kagwanja. "Refugee Camps or Cities? Camps in Northern Kenya." *Journal of Refugee Studies* 13, no. 2 (2000): 205–22.

Phillips, Melissa. "The Role and Impact of Humanitarian Assets in Refugee-Hosting countries." Working paper, New Issues in Refugee Research, no. 84, UNHCR, 2003.

Reeds, Barbara. *Assessing Refugee Self-Reliance: A Food Economy Assessment. Kountaya and Telikoro Refugee Camps, Kissidougou, Guinea.* UNHCR Evaluation and Policy Unit Background Document, October 31, 2002.

Rutinwa, Bonaventure. "Prima Facie Status and Refugee Protection." Working paper, New Issues in Refugee Research, no. 69, UNHCR, 2002.

Smith, Merrill. "Introduction to the World Refugee Survey." *World Refugee Survey, 2004.* Washington, DC: U.S. Committee for Refugees and Immigrants. www.refugees.org/wrs04/main.html.

Sommers, Marc. *Fear in Bongoland: Burundi Refugees in Urban Tanzania.* New York: Berghahn Books, 2001.

Sørensen, Nina Nyberg. "The Development Dimension of Migrant Remittances." Migration Policy Research Working Paper No. 1, IOM, 2004.

Sørensen, Nina, and Nicholas Van Hear, eds. *The Migration-Development Nexus.* New York and Geneva: The United Nations and the International Organization for Migration, 2003.

Sperl, Stefan. *Evaluation of UNHCR's Policy on Refugees in Urban Areas: A Case Study Review of Cairo*, report for UNHCR Evaluation and Policy Unit, June 2001.

———. "International Refugee Aid and Social Change in Northern Mali." Working paper, New Issues in Refugee Research, no. 22, UNHCR, 2000.

Stedman, Stephen John, and Fred Tanner, eds. *Refugee Manipulation: War, Politics, and the Abuse of Human Suffering.* Washington, DC: Brookings Institution Press, 2003.

Sussman, David D. "The Impact of Remitting upon the Self-Sufficiency of Immigrants in Boston." M.A.L.D. thesis, Fletcher School of Law and Diplomacy, Tufts University, Medford, MA, May 2004.

Terry, Fiona. *Condemned to Repeat? The Paradox of Humanitarian Action.* Ithaca and London: Cornell University Press, 2002.

Titus, Sarah. "CORD Microcredit Programs for Refugees, Nangweshi, Zambia." Alchemy Project Country Report No. 8, August 2004. www.famine.tufts.edu/pdf/alchemy/2004_8_zambia.pdf.

U.S. Committee for Refugees (USCR). *Pakistan: Afghan Refugees Shunned and Scorned.* Washington, DC, September 2001.

U.S. Committee of Refugees and Immigrants (USCRI), *World Refugee Survey, 2004*, Washington, DC, 2004. www.refugees.org/wrs04/main.html.

Van Hear, Nicholas. "'I Went As Far As My Money Would Take Me': Conflict, Forced Migration And Class." Paper prepared for the 8th IASFM Conference, Chiang Mai, Thailand, January 2003.

———. "Sustaining Societies under Strain: Remittances as a Form of Transnational Exchange in Sri Lanka and Ghana," in *New Approaches to Migration? Transnational Communities and the Transformation of Home*, edited by N. Al-Ali and K. Koser, 202–223. New York: Routledge, 2002.

Vincent, Marc, and Birgitte Sorensen. *Caught Between Borders: Response Strategies of the Internally Displaced*. London and Sterling, VA: Norwegian Refugee Council and Pluto Press, 2001.

Weaver, J. L. "Searching for Survival: Urban Ethiopian Refugees in Sudan." *Journal of Developing Areas* 22, no. 4 (1987/88): 457–75.

Werker, Eric. "Refugees in Kyangwali Settlement: Constraints on Economic Freedom." Refugee Law Project Working Paper No. 7, 2002.

Willems, Roos. "The Refugee Experience: Forced Migration and Social Networks In Dar Es Salaam, Tanzania." PhD diss., (Anthropology), Graduate School, University of Florida, 2003.

Wilson, T. *Microfinance during and After Armed Conflict: Lessons from Angola, Cambodia, Mozambique and Rwanda*. Durham, UK: Concern Worldwide and Springfield Centre for Business in Development, 2002.

Wright, George J. "ICAR Navigation Guide: Resettlement Programmes." Information Centre about Asylum and Refugees in the UK. London: Kings College, 2003. www.icar.org.uk/content/res/nav/keyiss.html.

Young, Helen, Yacob Aklilu, George Were, Andy Catley, Tim Leyland, Annalies Borrel, Angela Raven Roberts, Patrick Webb, Diane Holland, and Wendy Johnecheck. *Nutrition and Livelihoods in Situations of Conflict and Other Crises*. Medford, MA: Feinstein International Famine Center, Tufts University, 2002.

Zolberg, Aristide R., Astri Suhrke, and Sergio Aguayo, eds. *Escape from Violence: Conflict and the Refugee Crisis in the Developing World*. New York: Oxford University Press, 1989.

UNHCR Documents:

The Community Services Function in UNHCR: An Independent Evaluation. Report for UNHCR Evaluation and Policy Unit, March 1, 2003.

Evaluation of UNHCR Policy on Refugees in Urban Areas: A Case Review of New Delhi. Report for UNHCR Evaluation and Policy Unit, November 1, 2000.

Executive Committee of the High Commissioner's Programme. Protracted Refugee Situations. Standing Committee 30th Meeting, June 10, 2004. EC/54/SC/CRP.14. www.unhcr.ch/cgi-bin/texis/vtx/statistics.

Global Refugee Trends: Overview of Refugee Populations, New Arrivals, Durable Solutions, Asylum-Seekers and Other Persons of Concern to UNHCR. June 15, 2004.

"UNHCR's Policy and Practice Regarding Urban Refugees, A Discussion Paper," 1995.

"UNHCR, Refugee Livelihoods and Self-Reliance: A Brief History." Available under Research/Evaluation at www.unhcr.ch.

UNHCR Resettlement Handbook. Geneva: UNHCR, November 2004.

UNHCR Statistical Handbook 2001. Geneva: UNHCR, 2001. www.unhcr.ch/cgi -bin/texis/vtx/statistics.

Web Sites:

www.ecre.org

www.famine.tufts.edu

www.forcedmigration.org

www.more.fi

www.reliefweb.int

www.refugees.org/wrs04/main.html.

www.un.org/unrwa/programmes/mmp/overview.html

www.unhcr.ch

www.wfp.org

Index

A

About the Author

Karen Jacobsen is Visiting Associate Professor at Friedman School of Nutrition Science and Policy, Tufts University. She is also Visiting Associate Professor of International Diplomacy at Fletcher School of Law and Diplomacy, Tufts University. She is the author of numerous articles on refugee, migration, and security issues. In addition, Jacobsen is the Director of the Refugee and Forced Migration Program at Tufts. A key component of this program is the Alchemy Project, which conducts research on refugee livelihoods and helps provide funding and resources for livelihood programs in refugee camps and conflict-affected areas in Africa.

Also from Kumarian Press...

Humanitarianism, Refugee Issues, Political Economy

A Civil Republic
Beyond Capitalism and Nationalism
Severyn T. Bruyn

Building Democratic Institutions: Governance Reform in Developing Countries
G. Shabbir Cheema

Human Rights and Development
Peter Uvin

Nation-Building Unraveled? Aid, Peace, and Justice in Afghanistan
Edited by Antonio Donini, Norah Niland, and Karin Wermester

Protecting the Future: HIV Prevention, Care, and Support Among Displaced and War-Affected Populations
Wendy Holmes for the International Rescue Committee

The Charity of Nations: Humanitarian Action in a Calculating World
Ian Smillie and Larry Minear

War and Intervention: Issues for Contemporary Peace Operations
Michael V. Bhatia

Civil Society, Global Issues

Creating a Better World: Interpreting Global Civil Society
Edited by Rupert Taylor

Development NGOs and Labor Unions: Terms of Engagement
Edited by Alan Leather and Deborah Eade

Fighting Corruption in Developing Countries: Strategies and Analysis
Bertram I. Spector

Globalization and Social Exclusion: A Transformationalist Perspective
Ronaldo Munck

Worlds Apart: Civil Society and the Battle of Ethical Globalization
John Clark

Visit Kumarian Press at **www.kpbooks.com** or
call **toll-free 800.289.2664** for a complete catalog.

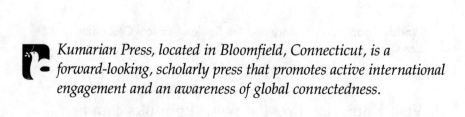
Kumarian Press, located in Bloomfield, Connecticut, is a forward-looking, scholarly press that promotes active international engagement and an awareness of global connectedness.